The Power of A Grace Perspective

By
Paul Ulasien

Technical Consultant
Dr. David Lawhorn, MD

INFINITY
PUBLISHING

ISBN 0-7414-6729-1

Printed in the United States of America

Published August 2011

INFINITY PUBLISHING
1094 New DeHaven Street, Suite 100
West Conshohocken, PA 19428-2713
Toll-free (877) BUY BOOK
Local Phone (610) 941-9999
Fax (610) 941-9959
Info@buybooksontheweb.com
www.buybooksontheweb.com

Acknowledgments

I can do all this through him who gives me strength.
(Philippians 4:13)

I would like to thank the following individuals for their inspiration and contributions toward making this book become a reality.

Dr. David Lawhorn
Sherry Ulasien
My Parents – Paul and Ella Ulasien
Catherine Weinaug
Sharilyn Grayson

Table of Contents

This book is dedicated
to the loving memory of my Katie girl.

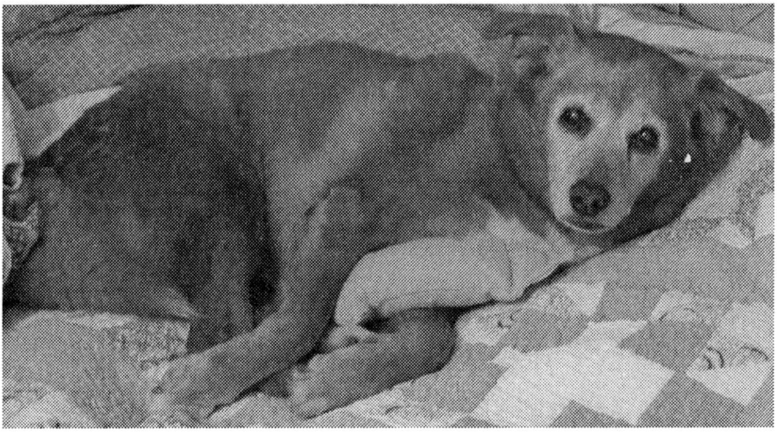

Chapter 1

Coming Full Circle, the Beginning

Uncharacteristically for a mid-August day in Kansas, I awoke to the unusually loud morning songs of finches, sparrows, and robins perched in the blaze maple tree just outside of the bedroom window. Typically at this time of the year, closed windows and whirring central air-conditioning units struggling to keep the hot and humid Kansas summer at bay muffle the morning songs of our indigenous birds. After several weeks of oppressive heat and humidity, a cool dry air mass had descended on the Central Plains just a few days prior.

Anyone who is from Kansas or who has ever spent time here during the dog days of summer knows how welcome such meteorological events can be. To me, however, this August day and the unusually cool weather that it brought meant more than just a welcome break from the summer heat. This particular Sunday morning was a day of coming full circle, as two divergent and wandering paths in my life, the paths of my spiritual and physical awakening, joined into one.

The central theme of the worship service at our church that Sunday morning was spiritual renewal through baptism. I had contemplated being re-baptized for many years, because my first experience of Christian baptism in 1962 as a child of nine years of age sprang from fear rather than fulfillment. That event marked the beginning of my wandering spiritual path.

My years of contemplations had come to a head in April, just four months prior to this August morning, while lying in an Intensive Care Unit after several brushes with death. Walking into my church baptismal under my own power and unaided by supplemental oxygen was also an impetus to end my years of spiritual procrastination.

A simple forty-five-minute procedure that was supposed to be a piece of cake instead left me in severe respiratory failure for ten days, relying on machines to keep me alive. My condition was so dire and grave that all the major organs in my body except for my heart and brain shut down due to an acute lack of oxygen three times during this ten-day ordeal.

The doctors gave up on me and told my family to prepare for the inevitable. Instead of having the proverbial one foot in the grave, just about the only part of my body that was not in the grave may have been a single pinky finger clinging to my only chance for survival: God's grace through a string of miracles. However, God's grace and his string of miracles while I was on life support were only the beginning of my journey. After regaining consciousness, I found that he had even more in store for me. Once God gained my undivided attention, he performed perhaps the greatest of all his miracles by granting me the perspective on how to make the best of my set of circumstances.

Cheating death and coming full circle to be rebaptized that Sunday morning was not, however, pure luck or a futile attempt to cop a plea bargain with God to save my life just one more time. That crisis prompted me to realize that for too many years I neglected both my faith and my health with decisions of indifference. I was not necessarily oblivious to the calls of my soul and body for action, but as many of us do, I always thought I could get around to it later, right? My brush with death that preceding April was a stark reminder that, as time goes on, we eventually run out of all of those "laters."

My path of physical awakening, however, began many years prior. In fact, that path goes back to my teen years, when I made decisions and dabbled in behavior that over time would culminate in my ten days at the brink of death in an ICU.

During the 1970s, smoking and drinking were considered cool, and most people did. Unbeknownst to me, however, I had a family history of substance abuse, whether alcohol, drugs, or nicotine. My heritage, as wonderful and diverse as it was, nearly became the figurative nail that sealed my coffin shut.

As I stood at the pulpit that August morning to tell my story to the congregation in attendance and then walked down the baptismal steps moments later, I came to a stark realization. God had not intentionally put me through my brush with death as a way of getting me on track. That was my doing. However, while he had my undivided attention, he did bless me with the foresight as to how I could take advantage of the situation that I created. Because of my experiences, I can share with others the choice of a positive perspective that I gained. God had intended that I write this book and my story all along, and he used my circumstances to accomplish his intentions for me.

Contrary to the teachings of my early upbringing that everything in life occurs according to the plan God predetermined for us before creation, my decisions alone determined this story, and God's faith in me allows me to share it with you. This story is not borne from some omnipotent predestination. God gave us free will because, if he did not, we would be mindless robots following a preprogrammed script of life.

Although God may have a plan and a path for us to follow, whether or how we follow depends upon the decisions that we make. God's grand plan for us is bigger than we could ever imagine or accomplish in a lifetime. It allows for free will in making decisions and gives us plenty of wiggle room for alternate paths to follow.

The ability to accomplish all the possibilities he has planned for us may be daunting, but the opportunities to do so are not. Every decision that we make may put us on to another path, but God will create new opportunities for every new path we choose to take.

Chapter 2

The Spiritual Balance Sheet

I remember the chuckles that I received one Sunday morning during a membership class at First Baptist Church, when the teacher asked me to discuss my religious upbringing. I began a lengthy oral dissertation that went something like this:

"Well, let's see, when my parents came to this country in 1950 from Europe, my father was Russian Orthodox and my mother was Lutheran. After I was born, they converted to the Assemblies of God. Then a few years later, they joined the Pentecostal Church, then the Holiness Church, and then a small group of closed-minded and misguided people called the Branham Tabernacle. When I turned eighteen, I said, 'To heck with all this,' and stopped going to church altogether until my first marriage, when I joined wife #1's church, the Disciples of Christ. I stayed in that denomination through wife #2 and into wife #3. We then moved to Lawrence and joined the Free Methodists. I became disillusioned with them after five Pastors in five years; so I thought I'd stop off here at First Baptist for awhile before moving on to something else. I figure that I still have stops to make at the Presbyterians, United Methodists, Episcopalians, Unitarians, plus whoever else I have time to join, because I'm going to make sure I have all my bases covered before I die!"

I was kidding, of course, as I made light about covering all of my bases, but I was not kidding about the journey of how I arrived in that class. Yes, I have taken quite a journey from spiritual fear, confusion, and disillusionment in my early years to a genuine search for fulfillment, peace, and grace in my later years.

The Fear Factor

As a child of immigrants, my spiritual upbringing relied on an abject fear of God and his wrath if I did not keep my life tilted towards the positive side of **the spiritual balance sheet.** This fear factor did not describe how my parents desired to live. The theology of the times coupled with the horrors my parents experienced during World War II and their personal tragedies during the war and in its aftermath helped shape their fear-centered thinking. Desperate to stave off retribution from God, my parents believed that their actions would determine their spiritual fates and that God's wrath would descend upon them if they did not keep it in balance.

My father's spiritual balance sheet began during the early stages of World War II. The son of Belarus farmers, my father was taken from his family in 1941 at the young age of twenty-one by Nazi partisans to work as a laborer in Germany.

Many times prior to my father's capture, he managed to avoid the snare of the Nazi partisans. Rumors had run rampant throughout the region of young men from neighboring villages voluntarily accepting partisan offers of factory and farm work only to disappear without a trace. Before each of the partisans' many sweeps of the surrounding villages, alarms spread from village to village and from house to house warning of the approach of men armed with rifles. The young men of the villages would then flee into the forests to avoid capture and wait there until the preying partisans left. More than once, only a few precious minutes stood between the first warning of the approaching captors and men with weapons kicking open the door of the house. Sometimes the partisans would make a sweep and then leave, and other times they would linger for days, watching and waiting for fugitives sneaking back into the villages for provisions.

Dad, on the other hand, was very self-sufficient and could win almost any standoff with the lurking partisans. I remember his stories of how, armed with only a knife and hatchet, he could live in the forest for weeks foraging for wild mushrooms, other edible morsels, and the occasional feral pig. This ongoing game of cat and mouse became a way of life and pride for him.

The partisans were limited to taking only one male member from each family. Although my grandfather had volunteered to be the one male taken, the partisans were more interested in young men who could endure the rigors of hard labor. The eldest and strongest of the four Ulasien brothers, my father was the primary object of his captor's efforts.

Dad used his youth and cunning to frustrate his pursuers until they decided to use these advantages against him. On one occasion, when he returned from a daring escapade into the forest, he found his mother weeping uncontrollably. In their frustration, the partisans informed my father's family that, upon their next return to the village, they would take either my father or all three of his younger brothers instead. The game was over. A few days later, Dad surrendered to his captors.

The scene must have been heart wrenching. Not knowing what to expect, the family and villagers convened at the Ulasien farm house to share a last meal and to say their goodbyes. Standing in the doorway as his captors waited outside, Dad turned one last time for a glimpse of his parents, who were anguished and forlorn. Little did he know that this last glimpse of his mother and father would be the final time he would ever see their faces.

The journey from tiny Maszuki, Belarus to Germany was long and arduous. Dad first had to walk several days under guard as the partisans stopped at other villages along the trek, gathering more men for the trip to Germany. Eventually the cache of laborers was large enough to warrant a truck ride to Minsk, where a train of freight cars awaited them. My father and the group of young men who had arrived with him quickly boarded one of the freight cars; however, now not armed partisans but armed German soldiers guarded them. As the door slid shut behind the young men, they heard the door locking with a rumble of bolts and the train's steam whistle screeching shrilly, and then they felt the jerk of the locomotive as it pulled out of the station.

At all hours of the following nights and days, the train made many other stops. At subsequent stops, however, joining the sounds of German soldiers shouting orders were the shouts and cries of women and children. The freight cars had no windows, but my father and the others peered through cracks in the wood slats of the freight car to get a glimpse of the commotion at each stop. The shouts from women and children continuing after the train pulled away from the stations told the laborers that the occupants of the other freight cars were more than just male workers headed for Germany.

At one of these stops, the doors of the freight cars banged open, and armed soldiers ordered all the occupants of the train to disembark on to a waiting platform. The soldiers quickly led the women and children and other men, all with yellow patches on their clothing, across several tracks and loaded them into another waiting train; however, this train was heading in the opposite direction of the one they had just left.

The German soldiers in drab greenish grey uniforms like the ones that were stationed at each of the previous stops ordered my father and the remaining young men from his train to line up shoulder to shoulder on the train station platform. Then those soldiers transferred the prisoners to other soldiers in black uniforms wearing peculiar-looking white, red, and black armbands. Starting at one end, the new soldiers counted down the line of men standing shoulder to shoulder until they came within one or two men from my father and then abruptly stopped the count. The men who were counted were hurried into the remaining cars of the freight train loading the women, children, and men with the yellow patches. The uncounted, who included my father, re-boarded the train on which they had originally arrived and pulled away from the station.

Dad and the man next to him, Stephan, who became his lifelong friend, learned later that the count which ended just one or two souls from them selected laborers to work at the Nazi death camps. Those unfortunate souls also most likely perished there.

Dad and Stephan continued by train to a little farm village in far western Germany called Grossvillars, the home of farmers George and Rosa Lieb, their sons Rudi, Herbert, and Arno, and their daughter Ella, my mother. My father's arrival at the Lieb family farm would also mark the beginning of **a balance sheet** for my mother.

Heartache and Sorrow

My parents never discussed in depth with my sisters and me the details of their relationship between my father's arrival at my grandparents' farm and their marriage. However, they openly spoke of the events outside their relationship, the horrors of life in Germany during World War II. My mother always referred to the period between my father's arrival at the Lieb farm in 1941 and my parents' application for emigration to the United States in 1948 as a time of "heartache and sorrow." Heartache and sorrow filled this time for my parents and their immediate family.

The German army drafted all three of Mom's brothers. The German Army's Waffen- SS recruited Uncle Rudi, a tall, handsome, and intelligent young man. Most young men of above-average height and stature received consideration to serve in the Waffen-SS. No one in Mom's family knew much of the details or actions of the SS and its various factions, only that to volunteer and be accepted into its ranks was considered a high honor, an honor much like service in the Army Rangers or Navy Seals would be for an American family.

Fortunately for our family's legacy, the Waffen-SS were elite combat troops involved in direct combat activities. To the best of our knowledge, the Waffen-SS and my Uncle Rudi were not associated with the SS-TV (Skull Units) which perpetrated the horrors of the Nazi death camps. Towards the middle of the war, in early 1942, Rudi was reported missing in action during combat on the eastern front, a status that even today remains unchanged.

Uncle Herbert did not have the same physical stature of his brother Rudi. Herbert, stouter than he was tall, was better suited for infantry duty in the army, and he volunteered to serve as a foot soldier. Herbert's unit fought in part of the back and forth series of battles in the North African Campaign. During the first battle of El Alamein in North Egypt, Uncle Herbert's infantry unit came under the assault of a fierce Allied artillery barrage. Still reeling from the heartache of Rudi's missing in action status, my mother's family, only a few short months later in August of 1942, received the news that Herbert had been killed in action and buried near the Egyptian coastal city of Alexandria.

After the tragic year of 1942, the Lieb family hoped that the worst was behind them. However, in early 1943, Grandma Rosa's health began to deteriorate rapidly. A visit to a hospital in the neighboring town of Bretten revealed that my grandmother had ovarian cancer, which had metastasized into several nearby abdominal organs. Within a few short weeks of the original diagnosis, Grandma Rosa died of complications of cancer and was buried in the family plot on a hill overlooking the village.

The personal tragedies in my mother's family abated somewhat during the remainder of 1943, 1944, and up to the end of the war in May of 1945. Mom's last remaining sibling, Arno, survived the war and returned to the family farm after the cessation of hostilities. However, post-traumatic stress disorder had already claimed Arno's mental state, and he returned home to a life of despair until he died of acute alcoholism in 1969.

The war may have been over on paper, but the collateral impact of hate and anguish were not. Regardless of the cause of war or which nations are right or wrong, the brutality of war will fan flames of hatred that can span generations. The brutality that the Russian army visited on the German people as it advanced towards Berlin was no secret. The stories of brutal acts of Russian troops, just like the stories of brutal acts of all armies involved in the conflicts, polarized the population. Germans reviled Russians, Poles, Czechs, and other Slavic nationalities as barbaric and violent. When the news spread that a relationship had developed between my parents, a German girl and a Slavic man, the ethnic hatred of the barbarians from the east may have spilled over into an act of violence.

One morning in 1945, a few months after the end of the war, Dad and Grandpa George were walking out of the farmhouse towards the barn. In an instant, a single gunshot rang out. Dad fell to the ground for cover, as did my grandfather, but not to take cover alongside Dad. The gunshot mortally wounded Grandpa. The identity of the gunman lurking in the shadows, along with his intended target and his reason for shooting at my father and grandfather, to this day is still an unsolved mystery. However, enough was enough. In the ensuing two years, in constant fear for their lives and the lives of their two young daughters, Mom and Dad, who had married by that time, decided to start afresh. Two additional years of living in fear passed between 1948, the year that my parents filed immigration papers and 1950, the year they were allowed to enter the United States.

Dad had family connections in the US, with one uncle living in Chicago and another uncle and aunt living in

Kansas City, Kansas. During the two-year waiting period, my father learned through frequent correspondence with his relatives where his opportunities for finding work were greater. Based on that information, rather than actually traveling to Chicago, my parents decided to make a place called Kansas their final destination.

After enduring a long boat ride on the USS General Harry Taylor, a brush with a hurricane across the North Atlantic, and days on a slow train from New York City, Paul, Ella, Rosemarie, and Verena Ulasien arrived. They set up residence with Dad's uncle, Sam Lasen, in the Armourdale district of Kansas City, Kansas.

Unable to speak a word of English, Dad was able to find work only in the slaughterhouses and meat-packing factories that were prominent in the city during that era (hence Armourdale was named after the Armour Meat Company). The packing houses were a magnet for thousands of immigrants from Croatia, Yugoslavia, Russia, and Poland.

The young Ulasiens were settling into a new land and starting a new life. The troubles and tragedies that they had left across the Atlantic were now behind them as a distant memory until Friday, July 13, 1951.

After several weeks of unusually heavy rains, in the predawn hours of Friday, July 13, the levees of the Kansas River crumbled, and angry water began to pour into the lower bottoms areas of communities along the Kansas and Missouri River basins. Armourdale was one of those communities located in the flood plains of the river bottoms. Within minutes of being awakened in the early morning hours by the sirens of emergency vehicles, Sam Lasen and his relatives found water rushing down the street in front of their house.

With only the clothes on their backs, the Lasens and Ulasiens made a mad dash on foot towards the Seventh Street Bridge only two blocks away. By the time they reached the bridge, the flood waters were already waist deep. Because of the suddenness of the flood waters, my parents had no time to collect any personal belongings. All that they had brought with them from Germany and all the personal possessions that they had owned were lost, everything. Once again, 'heartache and sorrow' had found the Ulasiens as they faced the specter of starting again with no home, no clothes, and no possessions whatsoever. During this period of loss, Mom and Dad met George and Rose.

George and Rose came to the aid of their stricken neighbors through their church, the First Assembly of God. Because George was an immigrant from the same region as Dad, George could communicate and translate for my parents as they struggled to get assistance for food and shelter for themselves and their two young daughters. George and Rose also led Mom and Dad to abandon their Russian Orthodox and Lutheran upbringings to become born-again Christians. Dad also credited this Protestant conversion as the impetus to kick his heavy drinking.

Through all the intervening turmoil and tragedy that Mom and Dad had suffered since 1941, Dad had developed a severe dependency on alcohol. His drinking adversely impacted not only his health, but also his relationship with Mom. Dad said that the moment he rededicated his life to Christ, he was able to turn away from his destructive lifestyle with a new perspective on his life. This new found faith sustained my father for the rest of his life, and my mother followed suit.

As they had several times before, my parents once more bounced back from their latest setback. This time, however, things were different. The tragedies and setbacks that had dominated their relationship began to wane as distant memories. Influenced by the friendship and bond that they formed with George and Rose, they established a strong spiritual foundation on which they built a life of purpose through faith.

Soon after the flood waters receded, Dad, with George's assistance, found employment at one of the many railroads that were also a dominant employer in the area. Through hard work and perseverance, Mom and Dad quickly scrimped and saved for a down payment on their own house. In 1952, my sister Jenny was born, and thirteen months later in May of 1953, I arrived on the scene. Our immediate family was growing, as was our spiritual family. We joined and became active members of the First Assembly of God in Kansas City, Kansas. At this church our family found many a kindred spirit, as the location of the church was near the ethnic community of Strawberry Hill, the neighborhood of thousands of other immigrant families who had also converted to the Protestant faith.

The good times and good fortune that our family was experiencing, according to my father, were a direct result of our faith and adherence to God's laws and principles. He believed with all his heart that his years of tragedy and misfortune were a direct result of misguided faith in Catholicism and his abuse of alcohol. He was sure that God was punishing him for his sins. To his way of thinking, the evidence was apparent, because as soon as he abandoned his sinful ways, his fortunes and life changed for the better. God was no longer punishing him, and as long as he and his family remained faithful, all would be well.

All was well until November 1956. If you have been keeping track, by that time our family was six strong, counting Dad, Mom, Rosie, Verena, Jenny, and me, the baby of the family. Mom was also pregnant with a fifth child. To keep up with the needs of four children, soon to be five, my parents both had to work. Still fighting a language barrier, they struggled hard to make ends meet and to cover the obligations of a growing family, home, and work. Although they were prospering, they had little money available for anything beyond the basics of food, clothing, transportation, and the mortgage.

My older sister, Verena (Reenie), became ill in late October 1956. Not familiar with the healthcare system or public services available at the time, my parents were somewhat hesitant to seek medical attention, as they believed that Reenie had just caught a cold or flu that would pass with time. Reenie's condition, however, worsened to the point that she needed to be hospitalized. In the early morning hours of November 8, 1956, my sister Reenie died of complications brought on by diphtheria.

As could be expected, my parents were utterly devastated. Preoccupied with the struggles of making ends meet, they feared they may have missed an opportunity to prevent Reenie's death. Had they only known of the programs for child vaccination available at the public health clinic or through the Salvation Army for families who were of limited means or capabilities, perhaps they could have averted the tragedy of a lifetime, losing a child.

I was only three years old when Reenie died; so my recollection of her and the family at the time of her death are faint. I learned in my later years, however, that Mom went into a deep state of depression and miscarried what would have been their fifth child under the burden of Reenie's death and the culmination of years of "heartache and sorrow."

Dad never talked much about what happened immediately after and as a result of my sister's death, but I could always sense that he once again believed that God was punishing him and Mom. Whether it was punishment for being oblivious to the assistance available that could have prevented Reenie's death or something else, it did not matter. From this time forward until their deaths, my parents lived on a predication that we must pay forward for our sins. Anytime we broke God's laws or committed any of a plethora of sins, God would punish us for our actions. Growing up as children, we lived in constant fear that at any moment, God was going to punish us for any and everything that we did wrong.

This is how **the balance sheet** mentality of spiritual fulfillment worked. Unlike the balance sheet of a financial statement, where assets cannot be greater than your liabilities and vice versa, a spiritual balance sheet was always out of balance. Your virtuosity's column needed to exceed your transgression's column by as much as possible!

So the foundation of my spirituality was the fear of punishment by what I originally perceived as a retributive God if my balance sheet tilted in the wrong direction. As children, my siblings and I learned that the blessings of doing things that were pleasing in God's eyes were in fact, the avoidance of punishment. Our rewards, we were taught, waited in heaven, not on earth. So we should not expect to be blessed as a result of our good works. Our good works were merely the process of paying forward to avoid punishment.

Out of deference to my parents, however, I must state that their attitude towards God and faith were not solely a personal perspective but also reflected an attitude and belief of the times. Remember, an entire generation of people during the twentieth century knew of little else but "heartache and sorrow."

As calamitous as my parent's experiences were, Mom and Dad did not suffer alone. During their lifetime, the European economic crisis of the 1920s, the Great Depression of the 1930s, two World Wars, the Korean War, the Cold War, the Vietnam War and countless other conflicts and crises caused millions upon millions of similar or even greater tragedies. An entire generation of people worldwide suffered through an era of more bad times than good. Therefore, their attitudes of faith and spirituality predictably skewed towards living in fear of God rather than experiencing his grace.

This common hardship is more than likely the reason the calamities of the Bible dominated the religious teachings of my early days in Sunday school. The Great Flood; the destruction of Sodom and Gomorrah; the Israelites wandering in the desert for forty years; the trials of Job; the Great Tribulation; and the Apocalypse: all these stories exacerbated a fear my upbringing had already instilled into me, as such teaching did in the upbringing of a generation of evangelical Christian baby boomers.

So instilled in me was this fear of things being out of balance that anytime I consciously did something I knew was wrong or sinful I would immediately start praying to God for forgiveness. Being an ornery and mischievous child, I can imagine the prayer queues in heaven were probably cram-packed with requests for forgiveness from little Paul down in Kansas. God must have been saying to himself, "What kind of monster have I created on the Great Plains?" In reality, I was not extraordinarily bad, but all the perceived sins generated during my childhood provided the impetus for my continual cries for forgiveness. Watching TV, going to a movie, men with facial hair, women with short hair, makeup for either sex, education, short sleeves, reading books not of a spiritual content, ad infinitum, were all considered sinful and not pleasing in the eyes of God or tilting **the balance sheet** in the wrong direction.

Spiritual Meandering

My family changed churches quite a bit during my early years. My parents, especially Dad, seemed as though they were on a quest for complete spiritual immersion. George and Rose, who befriended my parents after the 1951 flood, also shared a similar quest. Both our families drifted from church to church until they came onto a group of believers from Jeffersonville, Indiana whose leader claimed to be the prophet Elijah of the end days according to the Old Testament book of Malachi. In the Branham Tabernacle, home church of Evangelist William Marion Branham, my wandering spiritual path began to unfold.

Once or twice a year, our family along with George and Rose's would make a pilgrimage to Jeffersonville to see and hear Brother Branham. Claiming supernatural powers as well as the secret knowledge of the seven seals in the book of Revelation, or as the believers claimed, the message for the end times, William Marion Branham was the epitome of the era's gloom-and-doom traveling evangelists. Many lost, naïve, and vulnerable souls gravitated to his ministry. His diatribes warned of the catastrophes that would befall those who did not accept his warnings and missed the Second Coming of Christ, better known as the rapture.

According to Branham, at the moment of the rapture, California would slide into the ocean. He never was specific as to which ocean, but I assumed that he meant the Pacific. The ensuing tsunami would breach the Continental Divide, creating beachfront property in Kansas. Monsters and beasts to dwarf the imagination of Hollywood and the comic books would crawl out of the crevices of an earth racked by massive earthquakes and volcanic eruptions to torment all those who were left behind. The antichrist (the Catholic Church) would force us all to have the number 666, also known as the mark of the beast, tattooed on our foreheads. You could refuse the mark of the beast, but then you could not work, buy, or sell anything. During this time also no rain would fall anywhere on the face of the earth, and the moon would turn as red as blood.

All this tragedy would crowd into the span of a seven-year tribulation. No one could die during this time, as the skeptics left behind were intended to suffer for rejecting Branham's message. However, he did offer a glimmer of hope. If you remained faithful through all the calamities of the tribulation and did not take the mark of the beast, you could then join the seven hundred chosen ones of the rapture, those who accepted Branham's message, in heaven for an eternity of worshipping God non-stop. These prophecies would be fulfilled by 1977 because, as Branham would punctuate in his messages, "Thus Saith the Lord," end of discussion! Sounds like loads of fun, eh?

So naturally during one of our biannual pilgrimages to Jeffersonville in 1962, when I had reached the ripe old age of nine and was literally scared to death, my father insisted I be baptized at the Branham Tabernacle before it was too late. Branham baptized me not in the name of the Father, the Son, and the Holy Spirit, but in the name of Jesus Christ. Being immersed in the name of the Father, the Son, and the Holy Spirit was Catholic and, according to Branham, would condemn me to an eternity in hell.

Amazingly, right after I was baptized in 1962, I began to ponder the logic of the religious doctrine that was being crammed into my head. Although my skepticism was also a mortal sin in the eyes of the Branham believers, I figured that my chances of making the chosen seven hundred of the rapture were slim to none anyway, so what the heck. I was going to start thinking for myself! Uh-oh, it looked like my **balance sheet** was starting to look a little off-balance.

Logic helped me to realize that California could not possibly slide into the ocean, be it Pacific, Atlantic, or whatever. Giant lizards and rolling blobs of alien goo were not going to come knocking down my door. All Catholics were not evil tattoo artists. Also, it would always be raining somewhere on the face of the earth, and the Bible said that the Second Coming of Christ would be as mysterious "as a thief in the night." So how could some self-proclaimed prophet have the inside track to know that it would occur by 1977?

Well believe it or not, today thousands worldwide still adhere to the generations-old message of William Marion Branham who died, by the way, in a tragic automobile accident in 1965. To this day and even though his prophecies were wrong, this small group of believers continues to refer to him as the prophet of the end times! Now you can see why I earlier referred to this small group of believers as closed-minded and misguided; they still are.

Whether I just rejected "the message," as my father liked to call it, or rebelled against it, I began to split away from my parent's beliefs during my teen years and strike out on my own. As my hormones began to rage, so too did my sense of curiosity. I started going to movies without being stricken down with boils and sores. Being of German descent, I acquired a taste for beer in my mid to late teens, becoming quite the party animal. Again, I did not contract leprosy, and the earth did not open beneath my malt-soaked feet to swallow me. Therefore, I saw no need to repent of my new-found debauchery. Instead I began to believe, for the wrong reasons, that omnipotent punishment for my evil ways was only a state of mind. So I kicked the party into high gear and began to have fun as only a mischievous adolescent like me could.

For the intervening years between adolescence and my mid-forties, I meandered many times back and forth, in and out of spiritual balance, generally for convenience. When I was down or going through bad times, like my two divorces or a serious illness, I would make half-hearted attempts to seek God and his divine intervention to get me out of the present set of circumstances. However, as always, I would eventually revert to my party-hardy ways of fun, frolic, and indifference.

Chapter 3

Lifting the Shroud of Indifference

During the 1980s and 1990s my immediate family, my wife and I and our sons Matt and Jon, attended church regularly while the boys were growing up. Sherry and I wanted to make sure that our boys had a good church upbringing, but from my perspective, something always seemed to be missing. I was going through the motions for the sake of the family, but I left any sense of a personal spiritual connection in the pews. I always believed that I had some type of a personal relationship with God, but that relationship came with no strings attached. Because God had bailed me out of many a jam in my life without my having to make any long-term commitments, why not just carry on with business as usual?

In February 1994 at the age of 69, Mom passed away, just a few days after suffering a massive stroke. I was always a Momma's boy who was very close to her, and consequently I was crushed. At the time of my mother's death, Sherry and I were also under the pressures of moving to a new city and building a new home. As anyone who has built a home can attest, the stress of building a home can in many instances rank closely behind something as tragic as the loss of a loved one. So heavy was the burden on me to cope with all the pressures of losing my mother and trying to deal with everything else that I could only find refuge inside a bottle of vodka.

I was no exception to the propensity towards alcoholism in my family, as I quickly plunged deeply into my own dependence on drink. Drinking helped me to get through the days and nights after Mom's funeral as well as the days leading up to the closing on our house. The stresses and pressures eventually waned, but unfortunately, my drinking did not. I had started on a slippery slope with no way of stopping. My dependencies occluded the path that God had intended me to follow, and I was obliviously falling into a deep abyss.

The feeling of trying to maneuver through rush hour traffic with a thick shroud over my head is the best way I can describe my life at that time. I was cognizant of my general whereabouts but felt like I was an accident ready to happen. The sober times would remind me of my predicament, but I would soon dull the dangers of my behavior with a couple of drinks of liquid courage.

I knew that I needed help, and after several failed attempts to gain control over my problem, I began to think about the prospects of copping yet another plea with God. One Sunday morning in 1996, sitting in a church service and feeling the effects of a lingering hangover, I began to pray to God to help me get my life back on track, because I felt lost and did not know where I was heading.

On that Sunday, I was feeling dazed during the weekly announcements portion of the service, not paying any particular attention, until I heard mention of a forty-eight-hour prayer vigil planned for the upcoming Easter weekend. Thinking that this vigil may be a good place to start finding my way, I signed up for a predawn half hour on Saturday morning to keep the prayer chain intact on the day before Easter.

Saturday morning came, as did my very early time slot for the prayer vigil. With Friday being my day to unwind after a hectic week, I usually greeted Saturday mornings with a mild to severe hangover. This Saturday morning was no exception. In spite of a dandy of a hangover, I fell out of bed and raced to church just in time for my portion of the vigil. Remembering the instructions of the Pastor that we were to spend the time in prayer and or reflection, plus not feeling quite up to snuff because of my pounding head, I decided I would just sit quietly (not a bad idea for a throbbing headache) during my thirty minutes and then go for some breakfast.

Somewhat bored and unable to meditate, I picked up one of the pew Bibles and unconsciously rifled through the pages. What happened next, however, was not what I was expecting. I randomly opened the Bible, but everything on that particular page was a complete blur. I kept blinking my eyes and adjusting the distance of the page back and forth, thinking that the time of the day and my post-inebriated condition was causing a focusing problem. Nevertheless, the page only became more blurred except for two words that stood out as though in bold text: **be alert** (Ephesians 6:18).

I flipped the pages backwards and forwards, but each subsequent page was like the initial one, a complete blur. As I returned repeatedly to the first page that I had opened in the Bible, all I could read were those two words in bold text: **be alert!** I was stupefied by what was happening, and for the first time in many years, I did not blow it off as some weird sort of happenstance. Someone was trying to tell me something, something very important. Those words were the beginning of the answer to my prayers of getting my life back on track, but in order to find the rest of the answer, I needed to **be alert**.

I could not **be alert**, however, if I continued to allow my dependency on chemical substances to dominate my consciousness. I needed to lift the thick shroud obscuring my view of the path that God wanted me to follow, but I could not do so until I had a stimulated and clear mind.

Be Alert - Stimulation

During this time I was a sales support engineer for a large telecommunications company, a job which required me to travel extensively both inside and outside of the Kansas City area. To occupy my time while traveling, I always listened to the radio, usually tuned to talk shows as I drove my car or the company car during business hours. One afternoon while driving to an appointment, I was listening to the background noise of a talk radio program when, during a brief advertising interlude, a commercial advertising evening adult classes in a degree program at a local university drew my attention. Admittedly, I had probably heard this same commercial at least five times over the course of an average day for maybe a hundred times in the past year. At this particular juncture in time, I had an overwhelming sensation of someone telling me to **be alert** and listen to what the commercial had to say.

I scribbled the toll-free telephone number on a notepad in the seat next to me and soon after dialed it on my cell phone. Ironically, the person who answered the phone informed me about a new session in business administration beginning in just three days. Through what I believed at the time to be a convenient set of coincidences, I completed all the paperwork, transcript transfers, and financial arrangements in time to join the class. The details all came together through providence as though I was meant to do exactly what I did at this particular point in time. **Being alert** somehow began to make sense to me now.

As lost as I was in spirit, I was in a similar way never able to focus on a clear path as to my goals for what I wanted to do in my life. My first foray into college in the 1970s produced an associate's degree in foreign languages that I took because I thought it would be easy, but then I never found the desire to use it. My next adventure into college came ten years later as I became interested in computers and received another associate's degree in computer technology. This time, I focused a bit more on the results and leveraged my second degree into a career as a computer and later a network engineer. I found relative success in my chosen vocation and progressed through the corporate ranks quite rapidly.

So why return to school again? I was finding success in my current chosen field of endeavor, and to get a degree in business administration seemed to have minimal relevance to my job. A degree in computer science would make more sense. Quite frankly, I had no idea at the time why I chose that degree, only the sense that it was something I had to do. Still, I wondered how this study would stimulate my mind.

The very first class in this business program, unbelievably, was Critical Thinking. To this day, Critical Thinking remains the most relevant class I have ever taken. I even teach it now and then at a local university. I felt like a bright light switched on inside my head. I was suddenly thinking about all types of possibilities that drew my interest outside of my current life and career. In a great rush, all the corners of my brain that had been dulled by years of chemical dependence were screaming to come alive and become a prominent part of my psyche. There was only one problem; I was still addicted to the alcohol which was stifling my mind's cries to be set loose.

Be Alert - Clarity

About eight weeks passed after I started to stimulate my mind, but the thick shroud of a chemical dependency still obscured my spiritual vision. My reliance on alcohol as sustenance for surviving the day began to permeate my academic endeavors much as it had done in my personal and family life. In the hour between the end of the work day and the start of class, I had plenty of time for a couple of shots of vodka on the rocks or straight from the bottle to take the edge off. The problem was, as many an alcoholic can attest, my new endeavors only gave me another excuse to have a drink. I began to arrive for class without the full capacities I needed, and drank more as a result. My mind was so clouded from my dependence on alcohol that I could not have been alert, regardless of my desire. God had to send me an angel to grab my attention before it was too late.

The angel that God chose to send me came in the form of my wife, Sherry. Unbeknownst to me, though the news should have not come as any surprise, Sherry had been suffering from my alcohol abuse as well. No, and thank God, I had never physically abused Sherry or the boys as a result of my continual drunkenness, but the emotional scars ran too deep for her and our sons to heal. Even though she had been making recent threats to leave me if I did not get things under control, I always took those threats as idle ones, never thinking that she was serious.

On July 12, 1996, I stopped after work at my favorite watering hole for a couple of drinks, but I stayed a bit longer than usual. A great deal of thunder and lightning that evening accompanied a line of severe thunderstorms approaching the area; so I made the excuse to stay at the bar awhile longer rather than venturing out and driving my van in the storms. A lull in the weather did not come for several hours, during which time I continued to sit and drink until I realized I had been away much later than I planned. I tied one on this night and big time. Around 8:00 pm, I miraculously navigated my van the mile or so home without killing myself or someone else. I stumbled into the house, making another spectacle of myself in front of Sherry and the boys and passing them without saying a word. I headed right into the bedroom, fell onto the bed, and literally passed out.

I knew that I had passed out because, as I was to learn the next morning, I had obliviously walked past Sherry and the boys while they were huddled in front of the TV monitoring an approaching storm that may be containing a tornado. The tornado warning sirens began blaring just moments after I had collapsed on the bed. Sherry and the boys rushed into the bedroom and tried desperately to wake me up to take cover with them, but I was unresponsive. They had to leave me on the bed and run to the basement while I snore away upstairs, insensible to what was happening. Fortunately, no tornado hit that night, and all was well – well, not quite. That episode and the angst that my family had felt because they had to leave me in harm's way when they could not wake me was the straw that broke the proverbial camel's back.

What happened as a result, however, was not what you may have been expecting. You may have thought that Sherry packed up the boys that night and headed to her mothers' home in Kansas City, the usual destination she would designate whenever we had an argument about my drinking. No, she didn't make good on that threat. What she did, however, is the reason I am convinced that God used my family as surrogate angels to help me **be alert** and **clear my mind**.

After the tornado warnings and storms passed, in the middle of the night Sherry went to the twenty-four-hour drug store and picked out the most loving card that she could find. She wrote in the card about how much she and the boys loved me, but also how they had been going through counseling to come to grips with my problem and a planned separation from me. Sherry also wrote that, as a last ditch effort, she had made me an appointment to see her counselor that following Monday. She hoped I could sense the pain I was causing them as a husband and daddy who was destroying himself before his family's eyes.

I saw the card on the nightstand next to my side of the bed as I awoke in another state of grogginess the next morning. I read the card, put it down, and looked over at my angel, who had cried herself to sleep the night before, exhausted and still sleeping. I have remained sober, never touching a drop or popping a pill to this day. Sure, I still needed many hours of counseling and the support of my wife and family, as no one can cease a lifetime of dependency like turning off a light. However, at that point in my life, the thick shroud of indifference caused by alcohol lifted, and I began to see everything around me in a way I had never seen it before. I began to see the path that God had wanted me to follow all these many years, and that path was one I never dreamed I would follow.

A string of successes I achieved as a network and technical specialist boosted me through the ranks of the telecommunications company where I was working, all the way up to the revered position of a regional emerging technology engineer. In that position, I was one of only three specialists in my field of technical expertise in the entire company of eighty thousand employees. For years I had only dreamed of having that title. Now hundreds of subordinate engineers looked up to me as the go-to guy for support and answers. I was also the front man for pitching technology solutions to some of the highest profile clients in the Fortune 100. My dream had come true, and I was living the life I thought that I was destined to live.

When I began to allow my mind to be **stimulated** and **cleared** from the effects of my dependency, however, something with respect to the nirvana that I was experiencing career wise started to look finite and shallow. In my first book, *The Corporate Rat Race: The Rats are Winning*, I wrote a chapter listing several steps on how to thrive in the corporate rat race. This chapter was called "Playing to your Strengths." Playing to your strengths begins with recognizing what true strengths are: talents and capabilities that have an equal proportion of ability and desire. Then it moves to cultivating new interests that may develop over time as you grow and mature. I had true strengths in the technical abilities that I possessed at the time, but as I was able to stimulate and clear my mind, I soon discovered I had an even greater interest and strength in teaching and writing. **Being alert** led me to discover what strengths had been lying dormant for those many years. God's plans that I use the gifts he had given to me caused me to take a mental one-hundred-eighty-degree turn from the path I thought I was to follow into the path that I now knew God wanted me to follow.

Everything began to fall into place over the next several years. I completed my studies and became the first of my generation of the Ulasien family to earn a four-year college degree. My alertness, however, did not stop there. I knew in order to gain the required credentials and credibility I needed to teach and write, I would also need to **stimulate** and **clear my mind** through graduate school. Again, all of the arrangements fell into place effortlessly so that I could continue to go in the direction that God wanted.

After graduation, I began to write my first book. Other writing opportunities for journals and magazines began to appear as well. Two years after grad school, I also began teaching as a lead faculty member for the University of Phoenix.

Setting my sights on new priorities and working towards them with respect to my career presented me with a minor problem. I absolutely loved my job at the telecommunications company. I considered it to be the best job and career period of my life in corporate America. I could have continued doing that job right on into eternity; I enjoyed it that much. But that decision would have delayed or derailed what God wanted me to do.

Just as details fell into place to **stimulate** and **clear my mind**, so too did circumstances fall into place by falling apart in my corporate life. Right before I completed my graduate school work, the job that I loved, the position of regional emerging technology engineer, was eliminated because of cuts and restructuring. The company reassigned me to one of the subordinate positions that I once supported, and almost overnight I went from loving my work to hating it.

I was heartbroken and miserable. Every attempt I made to transfer to other positions that I knew would make me happier met with failure. And as I seemed to be sliding into oblivion, I slipped into depression. No matter what I tried to remove me from that miserable set of circumstances, nothing worked. I prayed and pleaded with God to help me out of my misery, and although he did not work as I expected, he once again answered my prayers. After ten years of joy and satisfaction and two years of misery and disappointment, I learned that my job was once more eliminated, but this time, so was I.

The author Ursula K. Le Guin once wrote,

> *"It is good to have an end to journey toward,*
> *But it is the journey that matters in the end."*[1]

Although the last brick in God's path had been laid, the time had now come to walk it. What transpired over the twelve months from the day I left my job to that cool summer day in August when I was rebaptized unfolded as the most meaningful journey of my life. After a lifetime of looking for God's love in a **balance sheet** and through the indifference of convenience, I was about to start on a journey that showed how God's love requires us to meet the simplest of terms; it's completely **unconditional.**

Chapter 4

The Easy Way Out

As I began to set my spiritual house in order, I was still struggling with the collateral effect of the years of dependency on alcohol. Everyone who knew me back in those days of partying and revelry could attest to the fact that during those times I was a low-stress, easygoing kind of a guy. But the reason I was so calm was that whenever stress and anxiety would ratchet themselves up I would just mellow out by getting drunk or smoking a cigarette. My simple way of coping with any potential problem was just to enjoy a few beers, have a smoke, and relax.

As is typical of people who engaged in this type of lifestyle, I also enjoyed my menthol cigarettes with my beer and did not worry about any of the ill effects such behavior would create. I was young, healthy, and active; so the looming specters of lung, heart, or liver disease were what someone else would get, not me!

Adding fuel to the fire was the fact that I also worked around a great deal of hazardous materials for a period of nine years. From 1978 to 1987, I worked in the coal yards of a power plant. Even though I usually wore protective masks to filter the coal dust and fly ash that was part of the work environment, I still inhaled these substances many times without protection. Our company gave us yearly physical exams to screen for black lung and other respiratory diseases. Each year my screenings always tested negative; so no worries from me. I enjoyed my smokes and drinks and did not sweat the dangers.

Working at the power plant was the perfect job for a low-stress person like me. I was part of a bargaining unit that gave my fellow workers and me top wages and good job security. Also, because the fuel/coal yards were located away from the main plant, we were kind of out of sight and out of mind. As long as adequate amounts of coal fueled the plant, no one cared what we did. With that freedom in mind, we goofed off much of the time! As part of our ritual of goofing off, three or four of us would go out for lunch and slam down a twelve-pack of beer to help us cruise through the afternoon. When the work was done, we would sneak off to our secret hiding places and catch a snooze. After work, we headed back to the liquor store to stock up on our supply of booze for the evening. What a life of nirvana for a low stress guy!

My life was not completely peachy, though. During this period of time, I also was married and divorced twice. My second marriage, which produced my oldest son Matt, ended in divorce when he was only eighteen months old. For a low-stress kind of a guy, dealing with divorce and the loss of my baby boy was anything but low stress. I made a couple of half-hearted attempts to reconcile my behavior with God, using the balance sheet mentality of justifying my problems. However, when my circumstances did not change as a result of my efforts to cop a plea, I would return to the thing I knew could help me cope: booze.

Fortunately, in 1983 I met and married the love of my life, my wife Sherry. The reason this marriage was fortunate was not that she was able to convince me to change my behavior, although she did later in our marriage. It was fortunate, however, because she encouraged me to look beyond my present set of circumstances to see that I had the potential to be so much more. Although my job at the power plant provided a good living for Sherry and me and our newborn son, I began to realize that I could be doing so much more. With Sherry's encouragement and support, I subsequently returned to night school for the degree in computer technology. In 1987 I left the power plant fuel yards and my party comrades to pursue a new career.

My parents thought I was nuts to leave the security of the power plant job. To tell you the truth, I was a bit apprehensive myself. However, considering the risks my parents undertook to leave their homeland back when they were trying to start a new life, they should not have been surprised by my decision to take a risk as well.

Although my risk had its rewards, it also had its consequences. Suddenly I began to experience as part of my job a new beast that I had not tamed for over a decade: stress. Even though I had stopped smoking cigarettes the year before I left the power plant, I substituted other things to calm my new-found stress. My drinking increased exponentially as I was unable to shake the few bad habits I inherited from the out of sight, out of mind days at the plant. I still liked to sneak out at lunch for a drink, only now I was drinking in solitude.

One of the negative side effects of heavy drinking is a lowered immunity to disease and infection. I always considered myself to be in relatively good health because I rarely succumbed to seasonal colds or flu. During my annual physical exams, I always received a clean bill of health. Like most alcoholics, I always noted the medical reports of the health benefits of drinking and compartmentalized any of the negative aspects. My body, however, was trying to tell me otherwise, and in 1990, it did so with a vengeance.

In the fall of 1990, I suddenly developed a serious infection in an embarrassing location which I will leave unnamed. Nonetheless, this affliction would consume me for the next nine months, culminating in three surgeries and two hospital stays. As I was to learn later, my excessive drinking had lowered my body's resistance to infections, preventing me from overcoming this illness more quickly. The double edged sword of stress was also involved.

The economy was in a deep recession at the time, and as a result, my wife lost her job a few months before I became ill. As we were accustomed to living the lifestyle of a two income family, we could not have lost Sherry's income at a worse time. We also had gained custody of my oldest son from my previous marriage, an addition which, though happy and welcome, added fuel to the virtual stress fires burning in our home. So my solution to deal with all the above stress was more booze.

You see, I was getting high through the whole episode of the infection, except for the times that I was on antibiotics. Most if not all antibiotics come with specific instructions not to ingest alcohol but say nothing about smoking or other unhealthy outlets of stress. This loophole may have been good news for my stress but did little to alleviate my illness. I would get better during these periods of medication and no alcohol, but as soon as I was done with the ten days of dosage, I went right back to the bottle. Then the infection would reappear. My inability to rid myself of the lingering infection also put me into a state of depression. Going from never being sick a day in my life to enduring months of pain and sickness was not an ordeal that I was prepared to face.

However, after my third surgery, I did finally heal and return to a normal life.

I began to settle back into my usual routine of fun and frolic once the infection was finally cured. The stress began to subside as well. Over the next several months, Sherry and I both took giant leaps forward in our careers, finding our dream jobs. As a family, we began adjusting to having another child, as well as a new dog and cat under our care, and the stress and anxieties looked as though they were now all behind us.

Slowly but surely, though, Mr. Stress began to creep back into our lives. Sherry's new job was located in Topeka, Kansas, more than sixty miles from where we lived. I did not want her to drive that far back and forth every day; so we began thinking about alternatives. Because my new dream job was also about a forty-five-mile drive, we decided to move to Lawrence, Kansas, in order to cut by half the distance each of us would have to drive.

Selling a house, looking for a new home, moving a houseful of possessions, and settling in a new city, however, are anything but stress free. Just selling our house took us over a year and a half. When we finally did, because we were so desperate to move, we agreed to the buyer's stipulation to take possession thirty days after closing. This agreement put us in a rather precarious situation. Closing day, as it turned out, was the day before Thanksgiving, meaning that we had to move the day after Christmas! We now had less than a month to find a place to live in a new city, pack all our belongings, and hire movers, all the while trying to create some semblance of a Christmas holiday for the boys!

So guess how I dealt with the situation? That's right; I turned to my old friend, booze, but now with a bit of a new twist. During my illness several months earlier, I had collected a ton of prescription pain medication. I discovered that washing down a few Vicodins with a couple of beers would take the edge off without giving me a hangover. Woohoo, the miracles of modern medicine!

I do not remember much from that period of thirty days, but somehow we were able to move and settle into a new place. As thirty days is not a great deal of time to find and buy a home, we were able to find only a rental home large enough to accommodate the Ulasiens and menagerie in relative comfort. We decided renting would be our best option, seeing that trying to buy or build a house in thirty days or less, was nearly impossible. This decision would also give us some time to scour the area thoroughly for a suitable location for our new residence. After a few months, we finally made the decision to build a new house.

If you recall from a previous chapter, anyone who has ever built a home can attest to the fact that supervising the building is anything but stress free. This chore alone has put many a good marriage on the rocks. In our situation, we also had to carry the burden of our grief over the unexpected death of my mother. Still reeling from the shock of my mother's death, we closed on our new house and moved about six weeks after the funeral.

Spending our last penny in savings for the down payment and cost overruns that are a usual byproduct of building a home left us flat broke! Enough stress already, right? Well, not quite! Because our closing and moving date also coincided with tax season, the IRS had a little surprise for us as well.

The year and a half that we lived in the rental home did not give us the mortgage and associated tax deductions that we normally enjoyed. Without these deductions, we painfully learned that we had underpaid our taxes the previous year to the tune of about $4,000, or about $3,999.99 more than we had. We had just sunk every last cent that we had into our new home, and we were flat broke. Therefore, as you can imagine, the stress and worries now facing us were enormous. Unfortunately, as before, I always returned to the same solution for coping with the stresses of life: get and stay as numb as possible.

During all the chaos, I developed a nasty cough due to cold that lasted for over a month. Not feeling well caused me to seek relief not only from medications but also from the euphoria of more and stronger doses of alcohol. Beer no longer satisfied my need for quick highs and quick stress relief; so I graduated to drinking vodka on the rocks with a twist of lime.

As time passed, our accountant arranged a payment plan so we could pay off our taxes over time. However, after a month of daily numbness to dull the stresses of building a new house, going broke, and losing my mother, I was already on a slippery slope of drinking myself into oblivion.

One Sunday afternoon, still not feeling well from my persistent cough and cold, I needed to do some yard work; so I took out the lawn mower and proceeded to mow the lawn. After about ten minutes of mowing, I suddenly experienced an excruciating, sharp pain on my right side about midway between my waist and shoulder. That sudden pain literally knocked me to my knees.

Thinking that I had pulled a muscle, I recovered long enough to go into the house to rest. The pain soon returned, and in addition, I began to feel flushed with fever and started to have difficulty breathing. Frightened, Sherry insisted we go to the emergency room at our local hospital. After an hour of examinations and x-rays, doctors determined I had pneumonia in both lungs that had progressed into a pleural effusion.

For those who are not familiar with that term, a pleural effusion is a medical condition whereby fluid accumulates in the pleural cavity which surrounds the lungs, making breathing difficult. Although in my case the condition was not life threatening, I was still bedridden for over two weeks with fever and shortness of breath. Heavily medicated with antibiotics as well as anti-inflammatory and pain pills, I did begin to feel better after about a week and slowly recovered. But for the first time I began to come to grips with how and why I got into the particular set of circumstances encompassing my illness.

Stress and alcohol had numbed my senses to the point that I was oblivious to the warning signs of my impending illness. I even hesitated to see the doctor because I knew he would put me on antibiotics that would require me to stop drinking! Besides, I had always been able to get over colds in the past; so why not this time?

As I lay in bed for almost two weeks, I had plenty of time to reflect on my choices. As a result, I completely abstained from alcohol for about four months. This sudden abstention falsely convinced me, however, that I could control my drinking and that I did not have a problem after all.

Anyone who has battled an addiction or has known anyone who has fought that battle knows abstention can plunge an addict further into his addictive behavior if he chooses to return to his indulgences. The body's response to ingesting substances such as alcohol diametrically opposes the brain's response. When a person takes alcohol or other addictive substances, the body elicits a decrease in pain sensitivity and increases a neutralizing tolerance to the substance. However, the brain responds to the numbness by increasing pain sensitivity and systemically countering the body's neutralization efforts. In other words, as the body builds its tolerance to the substance, the brain tells the body to ingest more and more of the substance to overcome the body's attempt to neutralize it. This battle of the body and the mind trying to "one up" the other explains how people become addicted to pain medications. Alcohol as an analgesic causes the body and mind to play the same tricks on each other.

In my case, the cycle started innocently with drinking a beer to quench my thirst after a hot afternoon of yard work. Rediscovering my long lost friend, my body increased its tolerance for alcohol, and my mind now wanted more than ever before to overcome the body's tolerances. As I mentioned in the previous chapter, my craving for anything to take the edge off my stress increased exponentially until that day in July 1996, when I became **alert** to my situation. Through the support of my family, my counselor Charlie, and the grace of God, my days of using alcohol to confront and alleviate the stresses ended as I **cleared my mind**.

Here endeth the lesson, right? Wrong! A person's ability to overcome a reliance on alcohol to cope with the stresses of life still leaves a great big five-hundred-pound gorilla sitting in the corner that one cannot ignore: the stress itself. Stress is a normal occurrence in life, and we all need to seek relief from it so that we don't succumb to it. Numerous maladies exist that medical science has attributed to stress. Some of these maladies are serious, such as heart disease, and some are not so serious, like just being grumpy when you become stressed.

Every day, problems confront us all. Depending on the seriousness of the problem, we subconsciously determine whether or not we have the emotional capacity to cope with the problem. The level of seriousness varies from person to person, as will the emotional capacity to cope. Some people have large emotional tanks from which to draw reserves of calm when coping with stressful situations. But others must supplement their emotional tanks with an additive that will boost their capacity for dealing with stress. For someone like me who had been relying on additives for most of his adult life, the emotional reserve tanks to deal with stressful situations, perceived or not, trend towards being small in capacity. Because those reserve tanks cannot handle stress adequately alone, if that person takes one additive away, he looks for another.

If you have ever seen a depiction or video of an Alcoholics Anonymous meeting, you may have noticed the participants chain smoking. The probable reason for their behavior is that taking the alcohol or drug additive away from their emotional tanks merely causes them to look for another additive: nicotine! When I said goodbye to alcohol, my body did not magically lose its craving for an additive. Buried deep within the receptors of my brain was the experience of the fulfillment, relaxation, and comfort that I received many years earlier from using tobacco products.

The switch began rather inconspicuously. In the fall of 1995, I was working on a project for a client in St. Cloud, Minnesota. One of the locals working with me invited me and a coworker, Lane, to spend an evening fishing for

Muskie (an indigenous fish) on the Mississippi River. Our host's fishing spot lay about one hundred twenty miles from the river's headwaters. Away from home with nothing to do, I thought the trip sounded like fun; so Lane and I accepted the invitation and met our host after work for an evening of fishing.

Before I continue, I'd like to warn anyone who has never fished for Muskie, as I had not, that a big surprise may be in store. As we three were stocking the boat prior to going out onto the river, I noticed that we loaded into the boat three five-gallon buckets containing lures. Each of these lures was at least twelve inches long and weighed over two pounds.

I am a Kansas boy, and in our neck of the woods, fish do not grow much bigger than the lures we were using in Minnesota. So I asked our host, "By the way, how big do Muskie get?"

"Oh, I once caught a Muskie that was eight feet long," he said as I gazed at the fourteen-foot-long aluminum boat I was about to board.

I then thought to myself, *Okay, here we are, three grown men getting into this little boat on a quest to catch the Loch Ness Monster!* That thought compelled me to ask another question which I immediately regretted asking: "By the way, does a Muskie have any teeth?" I should have seen our host's reply coming.

"Oh yeah, lots of them, and they're real sharp ones!" *Oh great!*

Thank God, the Muskie were not hungry that evening for lures or humans. After about an hour of not even getting a nibble, I was staring off my side of the boat into a general area where I was praying that no Muskie lurked. Suddenly I got a whiff of aromatic smoke coming from the back of the boat. "What are you smoking?" I asked our host.

"A cigar that I got from a local tobacco shop here in St. Cloud," was his reply. "You want one?"

"Sure, why not?" I said. With that, our host reached into his tackle box, pulled out a sterling silver cigar case, clipped the ends of two cigars, and handed them to Lane and me. Lighting up and taking a few puffs, I immediately began to enjoy the taste and aroma of this new found pleasure: premium cigars from the world of cigar aficionados.

With the exception of the night of my mother's funeral, when I was so despondent that I went out drinking with my buddies and smoked a cigarette, I had not smoked anything except for an occasional cheap drug store cigar for over ten years. This first introduction to fine cigars was innocent enough, I thought. At the time, premium cigars were becoming all the rage, with tobacconists and walk-in humidors popping up everywhere. Also, I discovered fine cigars in October 1995, about nine months prior to the day of **clearing my mind,** when I walked away from alcohol. So cigars were a fun hobby, regardless of how revolting my wife thought them. Besides, cigars seemed harmless, as aficionados did not inhale the smoke.

Funny how deficiencies and dependencies tended to lurk in the dark with respect to the additives I needed for my small emotional tank; I did not take long to become fully immersed into the world of fine tobacco and all the gadgets and accessories that attended it. I soon had them all: humidors; sterling silver clips, subscriptions to all the magazines, and a list of all the finer cigar shops within a fifty-mile radius. My new hobby was fun to explore and, I thought, harmless enough.

When the day of **clearing my mind** had come and gone, I soon discovered a convenient new additive that I could use in place of my old friend alcohol. All cigar smokers experience that one time when they accidentally suck a bit of smoke into their lungs. I happened to inhale a few times here and there, but after a while, the inhalation was no longer accidental.

For those of you like my wife and children who think that cigars are utterly revolting, the specter of inhaling such a revolting smoke must have been unthinkable. Remember, the taste or smell was not what enticed me, but my body craved the effect of the nicotine. This craving made me think that its source tasted good. We can apply the same principle to alcohol. Our minds try to trick our taste buds into thinking that an addictive substance tastes good as a rationalization for consumption. I remember the first time I tried beer; it tasted absolutely disgusting. Only after the first high I got from a beer did I convince myself that it tasted good.

Depending on my mood and the stress levels that hung over me, at first I could turn my cravings for cigars and inhaling their smoke off and on. For example, when my oldest son needed surgery for removal of a bone tumor, which thankfully was benign, I would inhale quite often as a calming additive to my emotional tank. Likewise, when vacation time arrived with all the highs and lows of getting there and back and the hustle and bustle of finding amusements and trying to relax, I made sure I had an ample supply of mild cigars to take the edge off my stress.

This on-again-off-again mode of smoking, which was at first more off than on, kept me going for several years, and my perceived control over it gave me no cause to think that cigars could get the best of me. As I mentioned in the previous chapter, since the late 1990s I had operated on cruise control in my life and career. I hit bumps in the road, such as the death of my mother and of my father three years afterwards. The same year as my father's funeral, my son Matt joined the Marines during a time of turmoil in the Middle East. However, other than these instances, I generally considered this period as the most peaceful and prosperous of my entire life. I was happy and thought that things could not get better. However, I always kept the possibility of all good things coming to an end in the back of my mind. I just had an overwhelming belief that such halcyon days would not last forever.

September 11, 2001 is a point in modern history that changed the lives of millions. In addition to the horrors and tragedies that we all had to face, the collateral impacts of 9/11 set into motion a series of events that would in some aspect touch practically everyone. If you recall, just prior to the 9/11 terrorist attacks, the US economy was beginning to show the signs of teetering rather precariously on the edge of recession. This imbalance arose in part because of the overheated spending and investing of the dot-com boom. And all those at telecommunications companies stood directly in the crosshairs of more bad times than good to come.

October 16, 2001 was a day that will live in infamy for thousands in my company. On that day, the first of a series of massive layoffs and periods of tumultuous change began. Eight thousand people lost their jobs that day, and for those who were left behind, the stress coming from the effects of additional layoffs devastated any semblance of morale. We existed in what seemed like a constant state of turmoil and upheaval. My position was reorganized, downsized, and transformed by the company eight times between October 16, 2001 and July 16, 2004, my last day there. The company was so chaotic at times that I was transferred between various departments and managers three times during one five-week period in 2002.

I read once that the leading sources of stress and anxiety are:

1. The death of a family member
2. Divorce
3. The loss of a job or being demoted to a lower, more menial position.

Having experienced the first two and faced number three, all I can say is that I concur.

I was fortunate not to have lost any pay or benefits as a result of the pending changes to my professional life; however, I do not think the actual loss would have mattered. One day I was one of the golden boys of the corporation only a few steps on the organizational chart from the CEO. The next day, I felt like an obscure nobody. A million things can go through your mind during times such as these, as well as in other situations of stress and anxiety. Nevertheless, you must somehow cope with the circumstances by whatever means that you have. For someone like me, a person with small reserves in his emotional tank, I needed to get my hands on whatever I could just to get through the day.

Through my faith and a great deal of prayer, I avoided falling back into the alcohol routine, but as time passed, I desperately needed another additive to help me cope. Nicotine was convenient enough as well as legal, and now my use of it increased exponentially. I switched to the small, filtered cigars that closely resembled cigarettes and smoked them in the same way and with the same frequency as I would have a cigarette. This habit, however, was only the beginning.

As 2002 progressed into 2003 and then to 2004, my career status deteriorated further and further. Every effort that I made to change my situation through transfers and promotion met only with more disappointment and unhappiness. I prayed and prayed, asking God to help me out of this situation by whatever means he could, yet I continued to slip deeper and deeper into what felt like an abyss.

One day in February of 2003, I was sitting in my cubicle, which felt more like a prison cell than an office. Suddenly, my heart began to pound in my chest, and I felt for a moment as though I was paralyzed. This symptom had never afflicted me before, and fortunately it subsided after about fifteen minutes. It did, however, cause me to seek professional help, and I made an appointment to see my doctor to find out what was happening to me.

Never having experienced such symptoms before, I was concerned. On the day of my appointment, my doctor did not take long to realize that I was suffering from anxiety attacks caused by depression.

DEPRESSION! That term had never applied to me, or at least so I thought. I always supposed that depression meant crying in seclusion and the like. I never imagined that anxiety attacks could also be a symptom and they could affect me! Nonetheless, my doctor started me on a regimen of mild anti-depressants, and after about a week or so, lo and behold, I began to feel better. The anxiety attacks subsided, and I felt as though maybe the worst was over. I weaned myself from the additive of anti-depressants, however, at the expense of an increasing reliance on a new additive, nicotine.

Even as my professional circumstances remained unchanged, I found other outlets to channel my emotions, outlets such as writing my first book, teaching as an adjunct at the University of Phoenix, and helping my son Jon to launch his career by promoting his music as well as starting a record company. Although I did not realize their benefit at the time, these channels that helped to keep me sane in light of my professional situation also served as the beginning of the answers to my prayers that God was putting into place.

The beginning of the end of my career at the telecommunications company arrived mercifully in early 2004. I had many friends in many places throughout the company, and little occurred within its back rooms that I did not know. One of these acquaintances was privy to the HR staffing strategies and called me in early March to relay some distressing news that she had just learned.

During the boom years of the Internet, the group of technical experts of which I was a member enjoyed the benefit of many financial incentives and rewards to stay with the company. This benefit would also be our eventual death knell. During cost-cutting meetings, the "excessive amount of compensation" my colleagues and I received alarmed upper management. They believed that they could replace us with equally talented professionals for less than half of what we were making. Consequently, we were all targeted for layoffs before the end of 2004, with one hitch. Because most of my group was also guaranteed rather sizable severance packages, our direct managers were encouraged to try to save the company money by any other means possible.

Saving money meant trying to get my colleagues and me to resign, thereby forfeiting the severance package, rather than be laid off. By any means possible meant a living hell for us. The stress of those means was too unbearable for about half my colleagues, who resigned prior to being laid off. For the remaining half, the end began to unfold by late spring of 2004 and came to an end by mid-summer, when the company relented and laid us off.

Also during that late spring to mid-summer, what began to unfold in my body was the sensation of becoming short of breath as well as experiencing pain as I tried to take deep breaths. Menial tasks such as yard work and chores around the house became more difficult as the year progressed. In June, I began to notice that something was wrong, just a couple of weeks before I was to leave my job.

My wife and I were driving our old classic convertible on I-70 in Missouri on our way to South Bend, Indiana for a national classic car meet and convention when we had a tire failure while going seventy-five mph. Luckily, I maintained control of the car and pulled over to the right shoulder of the Interstate.

After a minute or two while Sherry and I composed ourselves, I cautiously exited the car to assess the damage. The tread on the left front tire had completely separated, requiring me to replace it with the spare tire. Jacking the car up and changing a tire was something I had routinely done many times in my life. However, this time it was anything but a routine. As I attempted to remove the damaged tire and install the spare, I almost passed out from shortness of breath. I literally felt as though I was suffocating as I tried to breathe harder and harder but could not because of the pain that breathing was causing me. I had been short of breath many times before in my life due to being out of shape, but this time was different.

I managed to complete the repairs on the car, all the while not letting Sherry know that something was wrong. This kind of pain and faintness had never affected me before, but I did not want to alarm her. At this point in time, I realized something was not right with me physically.

The same thing but worse happened a few months later as Sherry and I took a short vacation to the Black Hills and Mount Rushmore in South Dakota. As I was walking up a flight of stairs at the Mount Rushmore parking garage, I once again became short of breath to the point of not only passing out, but also almost losing bladder control. I was able to stop and catch my breath, but now Sherry was becoming aware that something was wrong with me beyond what we could attribute to smoking.

As the stress and anxiety of being unemployed for the first time in my life was hovering over me daily, in spite of the warning signs that my body was trying to communicate to me, I continued to smoke those putrid filtered cigars at an ever-increasing rate. Not until January 2005, when I developed a severe cold that progressed yet again into pneumonia, did I finally gain the impetus to stop my nasty habit. However, by then whatever I did was too little too late.

Chapter 5

Something Does Not Look Right

I have always joked with friends and students about the two people you do not want to hear saying the word "oops": your surgeon and your pilot. From experience, I can now add the phrase "something does not look right," to the same joke.

Part of my doctor's examination and diagnosis process for my latest bout of pneumonia was a chest x-ray. I had been seeing the same doctor for over ten years, and he knew of my pleural effusion in 1994. With this history in mind, my family physician, Dr. Gravino, diligently and closely watched my lungs, as my earlier illnesses had caused a bit of scarring. During my annual physical two years prior to my second bout with pneumonia, he noticed a bit more scarring on my chest x-ray and decided to order a chest CAT scan. While he was not overly alarmed at what that CAT scan revealed, he did not hesitate this time to order another, as something did not look right on my latest chest x-ray. This new chest scan reinforced his concerns.

About a week after I had the chest scan, Dr. Gravino's nurse called, asking me to come for a consultation to discuss the results. The antibiotics prescribed for my pneumonia were doing the job. I felt much better, and my cough had almost completely subsided.

After I waited for a few minutes in the examination room, Dr. Gravino entered with an armful of x-rays, charts, and other reference material which he placed on the examination table. He sat down and looked at me for a few seconds without saying much of anything. He then uttered the words that I had heard before but never so somberly. "Well, Paul, something does not look right", he said. "The x-rays and chest scans are showing an increasing amount of scarring and possibly some fibrotic tissue, especially in your right lung. I think it would be best to have you consult with a lung specialist to see if he can make any sense out of all of this. I do not think it is anything like cancer, but something is there that you need to have a specialist see."

Whoa! Have you ever had that sinking feeling when you were expecting the worst and it turned out even worse than you expected? I had no idea what to make of what my doctor was telling me, and my speculations did not make a bit of difference anyway. The tone of his voice and the concern in his words were enough. For the past several years, my body had been trying to communicate to me that what I was doing to it through all my bad habits and through all the additives I was pouring into my emotional tank was bit by bit taking its toll. My problem was that I was not alert to the warning signs. I became so engrossed in the intervening stresses and anxieties of the past few years that I had forgotten about what God had tried to enforce in me almost ten years prior: **being alert.**

God lives in all things, in all of us, and he communicates to us through more than a spiritual medium. Erroneously, my alertness focused on a spiritual sojourn, looking for answers to my questions, while I ignored the physical warnings of what the Spirit was trying to tell me.

Coming from a spiritual balance-sheet background, I was accustomed to an environment in which believers prayed incessantly for God's healing touch for every malady from toothaches to cancer. Because of this orientation, many times I tended to look for the right answers in the wrong places.

I can remember from my childhood a particular instance when one of the brothers of the church had everyone weeping and wailing to God to heal his abscessed tooth. Back then, I was convinced that for such a godly man, a spirit would descend from the heavens to heal the poor brother's abscess, which by the way never happened. What descended from the heavens instead was probably God's voice yelling down to the poor brother, "Why are you bothering me with a toothache? Go see a dentist!" Just like me, the poor brother was so engrossed in seeking a spiritual solution to his problem that he was ignoring the obvious physical one. He and I were not **being alert** for the physical solution to our conditions, but that ignorance does not necessarily mean the spirit does not intervene to compensate.

Two years earlier while I was still employed by the telecommunications company, Sherry and I sensed from all the turmoil and uncertainty surrounding my job the need to make some changes. With benefits being curtailed due to cost cutting by the company, we thought that perhaps it would be a good idea to switch our health insurance coverage to the plan at her company. I truly believe, as we were to realize later, that this sense was not happenstance but another call to **being alert**. Making choices based upon that sensation of being alert was someone with a view of the big picture, God, trying to tell me something.

Six months had now passed since I left my job. Because Sherry and I had listened to the being alert sensations that we received two years prior, we did not have to bear the unthinkable burden of not having health insurance.

Moreover, as time and my story evolve, you will see how our alertness in this case was crucial to my survival.

Normally, modern day health insurance limits a patient's choices of medical care to the physicians who accept a particular insurance plan. In my case, no pulmonary doctors in my city or at our local hospital accepted our insurance plan; so I was referred to a pulmonary group in Kansas City, about forty miles east of us. This group consisted of two doctors, Dr. Howard and Dr. Fine, whom the insurance company highly recommended. Therefore, with my consent, Dr. Gravino made me an appointment with Dr. Howard.

Armed with all my x-rays, CAT scans, and other medical information, I traveled to my first consultation with Dr. Howard about a week later. I have to admit that Dr. Gravino's assurances that my problems were *probably* not a result of cancer still had me worried, as *probably* is not very definite. When Dr. Howard came to the same conclusion, I felt a bit more relieved, but that relief was short lived. Dr. Howard's next comment after, "It's not cancer," was, "Still, something does not look right here. I think we need to do a bronchoscopy."

In a bronchoscopy the doctor inserts a hollow flexible tube called a bronchoscope into the airways through the nose or mouth to provide a view of the airways and lung. He can also collect bronchial and/or lung secretions and perform a tissue biopsy. He does all of this, thankfully, while his patient is under sedation. Although apprehensive, I consented to this procedure and got a choice of dates and hospitals where the procedure could be done. I chose a date three weeks later and at the hospital nearest my home, which was more convenient for Sherry and me.

In the intervening time between my first consultation with Dr. Howard and the date of the bronchoscopy, I could tell that my condition was getting worse. Although I had inhaled my last lung full of cigar smoke about a month before, any exercise regimen that I tried to improve my breathing and lung capacity did not work. Whether I climbed up the stairs to my office or walked on the treadmill, any activity that required taking a deep breath caused me pain as well as a strange fluttering sensation in the upper right portion of my chest. Coughing, sneezing, and yawning also now produced increasing amounts of sharp pain along with the same fluttering sensation.

Normal walking was also now becoming a chore. I noticed that I had to go at a slower pace than before and that walking for any extended distance left me short of breath. Something was definitely wrong, and it was concerning me more each day.

The events on the day of my bronchoscopy turned out to be more involved than I had anticipated. Dr. Howard had also ordered a battery of other tests. Breathing tests, more x-rays, and an additional chest scan appeared on the schedule of the day all prior to the bronchoscopy. I was beginning to feel somewhat confident that all of this poking and prodding would reveal the answers as to what was wrong with me so that maybe I could get back to breathing normally. Still, I was a bit apprehensive about having a foreign object placed into my lungs probing around. Thank God for the sedation. As my wife told me on the ride back home, when the doctor took a biopsy sample during the bronchoscopy, I let out a big moan, indicating that it hurt. Thankfully, I did not remember this part, as I am a bit squeamish.

After I woke from the sedation following the bronchoscopy, Dr. Howard gave me a preliminary report on what he did and did not see. Dr. Howard was now ninety-eight percent sure that I did not have cancer, but he was still unsure as to what was causing my breathing problems. "The biopsy should tell us something," he said, "but in the interim, I want you to rest and use an albuterol inhalant whenever you are having breathing difficulties. In consequence of taking a biopsy, there is a slight chance of a pneumothorax (collapsed lung). This afternoon, you need to make an appointment with your family doctor for a chest x-ray to make sure that this has not happened." Still somewhat groggy, nodding was about all the reaction that I could muster; plus, I figured that Sherry would fill me in on the details once I perked up a bit.

I went to Dr. Gravino's office later that day for the prescribed chest x-ray, and all looked well: no collapsed lung. The remainder of the day and evening was uneventful with the exception of a bit of post-operative pain as a result of the bronchoscopy and the sedatives wearing off.

Recovery from the bronchoscopy progressed rather quickly. After a couple of days, I felt little to no discomfort from the procedure and was even able to play my trumpet along with our church's brass ensemble the very next Sunday, which happened to be Easter. However, playing my horn that day may have not been such a great idea. Beginning the next morning, my breathing took a turn for the worse. For the first time, I started using the albuterol inhaler, but it seemed to make my condition worse. A few minutes after inhaling, my heart began to race, and my breathing became laborious. I had no idea what was happening, and all

I could do was to sit quietly and hope that I would recover. After about an hour passed and things seemed to settle down, I chalked up what had happened as a reaction to the albuterol. Once again, I was not **being alert.**

Sherry traveled on business that week, and I felt reluctant to do anything until she got home. My hesitation, however, almost cost me more than I could afford a couple of days later. Once again I was having difficulty breathing; so I took another dose of the albuterol, hoping that this time I would not have the same reaction. Wrong! Once again my heart began to race, only this time it did so in conjunction with the chest fluttering and pain. Compounding my situation was the fact that I needed to leave for Kansas City to teach a class that night, and being old Mr. Reliable, I was determined to get there no matter what. My determination began to wane after about a mile of driving in the car as I began to feel worse. I immediately called Dr. Howard on my cell phone to tell him what had happened. I had not heard from him since the bronchoscopy about a week prior; so I thought that maybe he would also have some news about the results.

I had to leave a message for Dr. Howard to call me back because he was seeing other patients. I was still determined to get to class that night; so I kept driving in the hopes that sitting in the car for the forty-five-minute drive would give me enough time to recover from what I thought was an albuterol reaction. Dr. Howard did call me back about halfway into my drive, and I relayed to him what was happening to me. His answer was to wait until morning and to call again if I had not improved or if the problem got worse. And oh, by the way, all my tests showed that I did not have cancer, but otherwise he could not determine what was wrong with me. So I continued driving to class.

The distance from my parking spot in the school's parking lot into the building and to the elevator was about one hundred feet. For the first time in my life, I felt incapable of completing such a simple task as walking. Nevertheless, I somehow mustered the will to get out of the car, walk slowly into the building, take the elevator to the third floor, and walk another fifty feet to the classroom. To this day, I know that sheer determination was the only way that I was able to accomplish that task. At that time, getting to my classroom seemed to be the longest and most strenuous thing I had ever done. I remember looking around for places to fall as I took each step, hoping that I could call 911 on my cell phone if I collapsed. By the grace of God, I did reach the building and somehow taught the class.

Class ended, and though I managed to walk back to the car, drive home, and crawl into bed, I was too terrified to fall asleep. With Sherry out of town, what would I do in case I got worse, or who would notice my condition in the middle of the night? Therefore, I stayed awake all night watching movies, with my hand on the phone in the event that I had to call 911.

Morning finally did come, and I got precipitously worse. I called Dr. Howard as soon as his office opened, and he ordered me to check into the hospital immediately for another chest scan. Dr. Howard feared that I may have developed a pulmonary embolism or blood clot in my lung. Checking into the hospital is not something that you can do alone, especially in my condition. I called my father-in-law, Richard, and asked him to drive from Kansas City to pick me up and take me back to Kansas City so that I could check into the hospital. Like a dummy, I did not want to alarm my wife and interfere with her trip as it included an important meeting. I did have the presence of mind to call her and let her know what was going on but told her not to worry. That instruction fell on deaf ears, as she boarded the first plane home to be by my side.

That day and the next morning, I submitted to another round of tests, which found no embolism and produced only the same inconclusive results. In deference to the doctors, they did find that a part of my diaphragm which expanded and contracted my right lung was not moving, but yet again, this discovery was inconclusive as to the impact it had on the symptoms that I was experiencing.

Later in the afternoon, a cardio-thoracic surgeon by the name of Dr. Sams stopped by my room to see me. At the request of Dr. Howard, we consulted Dr. Sams as to what if any surgical options existed for me. Dr. Sams told me that he and Dr. Howard had decided they needed a lung biopsy to determine what was going on. Although Dr. Howard had taken a biopsy as part of the bronchoscopy, this type of biopsy would remove tissue from the outside of the lung through a series of small surgical incisions in the chest.

"Piece of cake," Dr. Sams said, "this procedure requires only three small incisions into your right side and should take no more than thirty to forty-five minutes tops. You'll need to have a chest tube in you for about twenty-four to forty-eight hours after the surgery to insure that your lung does not collapse, but after that, you'll be able to go home none the worse for wear." This procedure sounded simple enough and harmless. We made the appointment and scheduled the surgery, and because the surgery was not to occur until early the next week, the hospital discharged me to go home for the weekend.

Sherry and I were a bit apprehensive about the timing of this procedure, as it coincided with another of her business trips, which this time had her flying to Mexico City. We prodded Dr. Sams to discuss the expectations and risks of the proposed surgery, and he repeated, that it was going to be a piece of cake and that Sherry need not worry about it to the point of canceling her trip. Based upon this estimate, Sherry and I decided that she would travel as planned; besides, her parents and my sons Matt and Jon would be with me just in case. Even as we agreed that proceeding as planned was the best thing to do, something did not seem to be right about the plan.

I was nervous and agitated the entire weekend about our decisions. We had consulted what we thought to be some very brilliant and informed medical minds, but we did not consult the greatest mind of all, our God. Even though I was not feeling very well, I felt compelled to attend church the Sunday before my surgery, if for no other reason than to ask for God's presence and wisdom for the next few days.

Chapter 6

A String of Miracles

Miracle Number 1 – Being Alert

My surgery was scheduled for Tuesday afternoon at around 1:00 pm. I was, however, required to come the day before for pre-admitting and pre-surgical evaluations. During this visit, everything proceeded routinely until the anesthesiologist arrived. He began to read over the chart and rattle off in medical terms the procedure that I was about to have. As he read the file of surgical orders, I began a mental checklist on my own from what Dr. Sams said would be happening.

- "You'll be receiving a spinal cord tap to reduce the risk of movement during this procedure." **Check**
- "Dr. Sams will be making three incisions and inserting thoracoscopic devices for biopsy." **Check**
- "Possible lower lobe resection."

WHOA -- HOLD IT! STOP!

I felt a telepathic voice as plain as though it came from someone sitting next to me saying **"BE ALERT!"**

"Lower what?" I asked. "What is this lobe resection thing you just mentioned? I don't recall that term in any of my discussions with the doctors." I felt the telepathic voice saying again, "**BE ALERT;** ask more questions."

The anesthesiologist explained, "A resection of the lung means removal of any part or possibly the entire lung, and in this case it would be the lower lobe of the lung."

"This procedure sounds more serious than I was led to believe. How serious is it?" I kept asking. "You know, Dr. Sams assured my wife that this was a piece-of-cake-procedure, and based on that assurance, we decided that she should go ahead with her trip to Mexico City. If you were in my shoes, would you want your wife to be present for what you just described to me?"

"If it were me," he said, "Yes without a doubt, I would want her there."

"BE ALERT!"

To avoid an unpleasant situation, I could very easily have dismissed what this doctor was saying as minutia or just him being overly cautious. However, such an overwhelming feeling came over me at that point that I called for the surgical nurse and told her I could not go through this procedure without my wife present. The telepathic message to **be alert** was so compelling that a nurse's negative reaction or the counterargument of a hospital and its surgeons was of little importance. God was yelling down to me not to begin the surgery until Sherry returned home. As the events of the next week unfolded and I did finally go into surgery, Sherry and I realized that this **be alert** call was God's first miracle to save me from the brink of death.

The following Tuesday, April 12, 2005, was the scheduled date for my surgery and hospital stay. Sherry was now with me, and at 5:30 am, we drove the forty minutes to Kansas City, Kansas, where the hospital was located.

Because my original surgery had to be rescheduled, the hospital asked me to come earlier than my appointment time in the event that an opening appeared during the morning. Otherwise, I could expect my surgery to take place between 12:00 and 1:00 pm.

The earlier time never materialized; so we settled into a long wait. For a devoted coffee drinker, even a brief ten minutes waiting on coffee to brew can be an eternity, let alone a whole morning with no coffee at all! Prior to any surgery, the patient can take no solids or liquids orally after 6:00 pm the preceding day. Arrrghh, I was fidgety without my caffeine, but I was looking forward to having a cup of coffee later that afternoon after my surgery.

At around 11:00 am, a nurse adorned in surgical scrubs and carrying a chart called my name. Sherry and I followed her to the surgical prep room, where I donned my obligatory backside exposure gown and waited for the cocktail nurse to administer the pre-surgical concoction of feel-good drugs. Isn't that stuff amazing? One second you can be a nervous wreck, and the next you are cool, calm, and collected! Like I said before, woohoo, the miracles of modern medicine!

Only minutes seemed to pass after I received my feel-good injections, when the anesthesia nurse came to take me into surgery. Sherry and I kissed before the nurses wheeled me into the surgery room. I do remember seeing the bright lights of the room getting brighter as I slid over from the gurney onto the table. My last recollection was of everything fading away as I succumbed to the anesthesia.

From this point on, my story relies heavily on the accounts of those with me who witnessed the events of the next ten days.

An entourage of family members anxiously kept vigil in the waiting room for news from the nurses and or doctors. I use the term "entourage" because relatives on Sherry's side of the family will customarily arrive en masse to support others during times such as these. Accompanying Sherry as she waited for news about my surgery were her parents, Betty and Richard, along with her aunt and uncle, Virginia and Leroy. My sons Matt and Jon were working that day, and as this biopsy was a piece-of-cake-procedure, Sherry told them to go to work and come to see me later that evening.

As the hands of the waiting room clock continued to sweep in slow circles around its face, the casual conversations and idle chatter in the waiting room began to change to a more serious tone as thirty to forty-five minutes turned into sixty minutes, then ninety minutes, then one hundred twenty minutes, and then one hundred eighty minutes. After over three and a half hours, Dr. Sams finally emerged from the surgical suite. Dr. Sams asked for everyone to move into a private consulting room, and a nervous silence fell over the group as the door closed in behind them.

"First of all, your husband is doing fine and resting comfortably in the recovery room," Dr. Sams began. "I apologize for the delay and lack of updates, but we came across something unexpected when we began to take the biopsy with a thoracoscope. We were caught by surprise when we entered your husband's chest expecting to take a biopsy of his right lung, because his lung was not where we expected it to be. In fact, his right lung had collapsed into the upper portion of his pleural cavity," the doctor explained as he drew a diagram on the white board in the private room.

"His right lung was so diseased and scarred that we needed to make a quick decision, and we decided to perform surgery on his lung to:

A. Remove a portion of his right lung that was too diseased to continue normal function.

B. Remove as much scar tissue as we could from the remainder of his right lung.

C. Try to get his lung to resume its natural shape and position.

"That emergency is what took so long and why we did not come out earlier than we did. We did have to make a large incision through the ribs to perform this procedure. The good news is that after about ninety minutes of removing the diseased lobe and all the scar tissue, his lung dropped back into position and seems to be functioning normally. Because of the radical nature of what we had to do, we are going to keep him in Intensive Care overnight, and if all goes as we expect, we will move him into a regular room later tomorrow. Afterwards he should be able to go home in a couple of days. I just stopped to see him on my way out here, and he was already awake and joking with the nurses. So he is going to be fine." Dr. Sams looked around the room and asked, "Any questions?"

After a long oral dissertation like that, you could have heard a pin drop in that room, as everyone was dumbfounded. This news was not what they had expected, and although I seemed to be doing all right, their only reaction was silence resulting from shock.

True to Dr. Sams' word, I moved into the ICU and seemed to be recovering as he predicted I would. Still with a false sense of security and because I needed my rest, everyone stopped by the room early before leaving and then wished me well. Sherry hugged and kissed me before she left because I was tiring and said that she would come first thing in the morning before they moved me out of ICU. The last words that I heard from Sherry for the next ten days and almost for an eternity were, "Good night, sweetheart, I love you."

The phone at my home rang at around 4:00 am. "Mrs. Ulasien? This is the ICU nurse on duty at the hospital." For an instant, Sherry thought that she was dreaming. "There's no reason for alarm, I just wanted to let you know that your husband started to have a little difficulty breathing, and we placed him on a CPAP (continuous positive airway pressure) machine to help him breathe a little better. I don't think that you need to come. He's not in any trouble right now. I just thought I should let you know in case you came in later and saw this machine helping him to breathe."

"Are you sure that I don't need to come in?" replied Sherry, now fully awake.

"Oh no," the nurse said, "his vitals are stable; I just wanted to keep you informed."

"Okay," *(I guess),* Sherry warily replied and thought.

After that call, Sherry was not able to return to sleep. So she lay with our dog Katie on the living room couch, watching old movies and all the while thinking in the back of her mind: *Surely he's okay, or they would have told me to come, right? I'll just lay here awhile and then get dressed and drive into KC later.*

Matt, my eldest son, had started a new job just a couple of weeks prior to the morning after my surgery. Because his shift did not start until 11:00 am, he decided to come to see me before going to work. His visit is one of the last of the few recollections that I have of that morning, April 13, 2005. When Matt came to see me in the ICU, he had a worried look on his face. As he observed me laboring to breathe on the CPAP machine, he said, "Dad, are you okay? What's wrong?" As any parent can attest, seeing the look of fear and anguish on your child's face, no matter how young or old they may be, would normally be a cause to spring into action. However, at this moment I was incapable of providing the assurance and comfort that my son sought, because for the first time in my life, I realized that I was dying.

The CPAP machine was doing its job of forcing pure oxygen into the mask and my lungs, but during this brief moment of recollection, no matter how hard or how fast I tried to take in each breath, I was suffocating. Between breath cycles of the CPAP, I struggled to tell Matt, "I'm in trouble! Call Mom and tell her to get here right away!"

Matt, as any child would, felt the ice-cold chill of panic hit him like a ton of bricks. First he called home, but no one answered, leading to more panic. Next he called Sherry's cell phone, which rang and rang for what seemed like a hundred times before she answered.

"Hi, Hon," Sherry said, using her usual greeting to me and her boys, "what's up?"

"Mom, where are you? Something's wrong with Dad! I'm scared; I don't know what to do. He wants you to get here right away. I think he's in trouble," Matt said, his voice quivering.

"Matt, I'm on the turnpike right now, and I'll be there in just a few minutes," Sherry said reassuringly. "Don't worry, he'll be fine."

"Okay, Mom," Matt said. "Hurry, I don't know what to do."

Now Sherry began to realize that the call of a few hours earlier was a sign that maybe all was not right. She stepped harder on the accelerator and pushed her car way beyond the speed limit. As Sherry has a propensity to drive fast on a normal day, when she told me later that she went way beyond the speed limit, I imagined her torch-red car turning into a white-hot afterburner.

Fading in and out of consciousness, I do recall telling myself that I needed to be on a respirator because, as I labored so hard to breathe, I knew that I was going to die if I did not get any help. Whether or not I said so to anybody, I cannot recall. In addition, I also recall calling out to God during this time: *God, I'm scared; don't let me die.*

My son and, as I later learned, my father-in-law, while waiting for Sherry to arrive, were trying to call the nurse's attention to the fact that I was in trouble. Each time, the nurse would look at my vitals on the remote monitor and say, "He's stable; he just needs to relax and let the CPAP machine do its job." When Sherry arrived, the panic spread to her as well as she observed me laboring to breathe on the CPAP machine. I do not recall Sherry's arrival or presence, but as she described the scene to me, I was laboring so hard to breathe that my chest sunk and expanded severely enough to let her know that something had to be done and done now.

As you may recall from earlier in this chapter, the first of God's miracles during this entire experience occurred a week prior, when once again God told me to **be alert.** That miracle was when I felt his telepathic presence in the pre-surgical preparation room telling me not to begin the operation until Sherry was home. As we would come to realize, God needed

Sherry to stay with me so that, working through her, the exact right people at the exact right time would be in the exact right place to keep his string of miracles unbroken.

Miracle Number 2 – "Places, Everyone" Part I

Repeating what Matt and her father were trying to say, Sherry immediately rushed out to the ICU nursing station and told them that I was in trouble, but this time she told them to get the doctor. "We've already paged Dr. Howard and Dr. Sams. Dr. Sams is in surgery, but Dr. Howard should be here within the hour."

Sherry had the gut feeling that I did not have an hour. Going back into my ICU room, she looked at Richard and said, "Dad, I don't know what to do!"

Richard replied, "Maybe you should call David."

David Lawhorn and I have been the closest of friends since our junior high school days which, when put into perspective, is about three or four days after God created dirt. I jest! We have been through thick and thin times together and have always been there for each other. Even today, we live only a few blocks from one another. David, my lifelong friend, is also Dr. David, a tenacious and well-respected doctor of anesthesia who is married to Dr. Stephanie Lawhorn, an equally well-respected doctor of cardiology. Whenever we needed help and advice on a medical question or situation, we could always count on David to step up to the plate and take charge. Sherry had David's home phone number programmed into her cell phone; so she dialed it.

"David, this is Sherry. Something's not right with Paul. He's having trouble breathing, and we can't seem to get anyone to do anything."

"Well, I was getting into the car to drive into Kansas City to see him, and **I had this feeling** to check for my cell phone. I realized I forgot it; so I was just heading back into the house when I heard the home phone ringing. I was running to answer the phone before it went to voicemail; so pardon me if I sound out of breath," David panted as he also sensed panic in Sherry's tone of voice.

"David, how long will it be before you get here," pleaded Sherry.

"Not for about an hour; do you want me to talk to the nurse on staff?" he asked.

"Would you, please? I don't know what to do," she said.

"Put the nurse on the phone," David replied.

Because Sherry was on her cell phone, she asked David to hold on for a second, while she ran to the ICU's nursing station. She informed the nurse who was on the phone and gave her consent as the next of kin for the nurse to talk to David and give him information about my condition (we have so darn many regulations in place today to protect information that one cannot wonder as to these regulations getting in the way sometimes). David and the nurse on staff talked a few minutes as she read to him my vitals and conveyed my latest condition. After those few minutes, David apparently asked the nurse to give the phone back to Sherry.

When Sherry replied, "Yes" to David, all anyone could hear within thirty feet was David yelling at the top of his voice, "I DON'T CARE WHAT IT TAKES OR WHO YOU

HAVE TO GET IN THERE, BUT GET PAUL ON A RESPIRATOR STAT! YOU'RE LOSING HIM!"

At that precise moment, anyone who was working in the ICU and heard that command scream from the tiny cell phone speaker throughout the entire ward immediately shifted from his or her complacent, wait-and-see mode into full urgency. Within seconds, doctors, nurses, and respiratory therapists seemed to appear from nowhere, shoving everyone out of my room as they finally realized that I was within minutes of dying.

Here was my last conscious recollection. Even though I was suffocating and my body was hypoxic (starving for oxygen), I remember regarding the CPAP machine and the oxygen it was trying to feed into my lungs as my last and only conduit to life. When the doctor removed the mask to insert the endotracheal tube for the respirator, I remember flinging my arms wide and violently fighting for air as I had my last conscious thought: ***Oh God, please don't let me die.*** I then began fading away, not knowing if I was passing out or passing away.

Miracle Number 3 – "Places Everyone" Part II

Sherry and her father felt as though an eternity had passed. In actuality, from the time that they were hurriedly escorted from the ICU for the team of doctors and nurses to get me on the respirator and stabilized, almost two hours had gone by. As we discovered later, I had spiraled down so far towards the brink of death that morning that the team of physicians spent a majority of those two hours trying merely to keep me from dying.

As David later described this first critical episode, I not only had the proverbial one foot in the grave, but both feet, both legs, and both arms. About the only thing that I did not have in the grave was maybe my pinky finger clinging to the brink of life.

Anyone who called or stopped by the hospital to check on me only heard the ominous message, "Mr. Ulasien is in grave condition and cannot receive any visitors or messages." Moreover, this emergency was only the first critical episode.

Although I was somewhat stabilized, for the next five days, I endured at least two more episodes of nearing the brink of death. The doctors were repeatedly unsuccessful in trying to diagnose what was wrong with me. They resorted to experimenting with different treatment regimens to find an answer, any answer. One of these brink-of-death episodes occurred during a visit that David had decided to make to check on my condition.

With Sherry's permission, David was able to consult with my doctors and access any and all of my records and procedures. In addition, as the other doctors learned, David was vigilant with respect to the who-what-when-where-and-how of my diagnosis and treatment. Remember my earlier description of Dr. David as well-respected and tenacious? During a visit on my third day of being on the brink, God used David's tenacity as His vehicle for miracle number three.

You have probably deduced by now that my lungs were not functioning properly. This condition is called respiratory failure. Respiratory failure can manifest itself in one of two ways. One is ventilatory failure, in which the lungs are not strong enough to intake adequate amounts of oxygen, and the other (what I had) is hypoxemic respiratory failure, in which the lungs cannot process and pass enough oxygen to the blood, thus depriving the other organs, including the heart, of oxygen.

Depending on the amount of oxygen that the heart and other organs require, the heart will work in conjunction with the lungs to accelerate or slow the process of oxygen intake and blood circulation. Normal exercise is a good example of this relationship. When you are at rest, respiratory and heart rates will lower. When you exercise, however, you begin to breathe faster, and your heart begins to pump faster as the rate of oxygen that the body requires increases exponentially. That function is natural. What is not natural occurs when you are at rest and the body does not receive enough oxygen. The response of the heart is the same as in vigorous exercise; however, the result can be life threatening.

A condition known as tachycardia occurs when the body is at rest but the heart begins to beat rapidly. Tachycardia can harm the body in two ways. First, when the heart beats too rapidly, it may pump blood less efficiently. Second, the faster the heart beats, the more oxygen and nutrients the heart requires. This condition produces a vicious cycle. The heart wants more oxygen; so it beats faster. But if it beats too fast, it delivers oxygen less efficiently; so it starts to beat even faster.

With respect to my hypoxia and tachycardia, my attending physicians were using a process-of-elimination approach to finding out what was NOT wrong with me. Although that approach may not seem to be too out of the ordinary, in my case it was exacerbating my condition and keeping me at the brink of death. Enter my lifelong friend Dr. David, the tenacious!

Contrary to my attending physicians' approach of finding out what was NOT wrong with me, David knew that my condition was too tenuous for such a guessing game, and he had little to no patience for this approach. In cases of extreme conditions such as mine, David's training and experience have led him to the reality that the probabilities of survival for someone in a grave condition greatly decrease when the doctor is trying to find out what is NOT wrong with his patient. However, the probabilities of survival are greatly increase if the doctor focuses on trying to find out what IS wrong instead.

When David entered my ICU room, he was appalled to find that my tachycardia was producing a deadly heart rate of around two hundred beats per minute! In addition, he found as he examined my charts that I was also dehydrated, causing me to go into hypovolemic shock, a shock caused by low blood volume. I had also developed a pleural effusion, commonly known as water on the lungs, which in essence strangles the lungs. In addition, by looking at my charts David discovered that I was being administered an antibiotic mixed with an amphetamine-type stimulant to excite my nervous system. This concoction of drugs was causing my heart to race even faster, my blood volume to further decrease, my shock to increase, and my pleural areas to fill with even more fluid. Where were my doctors? Duh, nobody knew, and in fact, no one had seen them for several hours.

I can only imagine that **it** (and you can substitute any word you like for **it**) hit the fan, and to this day, David still cannot aptly describe the rage that filled him at that moment. Knowing David for these many years, I have seen him lose his cool a time or two, but as he described to me later, only God was going to stop him from kicking some tail around that ICU ward. Given that inclination, I think that even God probably stepped aside and let David do his thing.

You can probably deduce that David made no friends and probably a few enemies that day. He started with a vitriolic tongue lashing of the attending nurses for sitting on their haunches (I can guarantee David did not use the word haunches) while they watched my heart race at two hundred beats per minute and my lung functions decrease, yet did nothing nor sensed enough concern to call for assistance. That tongue lashing finally produced a call to one of my attending physicians, who quickly arrived only to get what the nurses got, however, at a thousand-fold. From what I learned later, quite an argument ensued not only between David and my attending physician, but also between my friend and the other physicians who were part and parcel of the experiments with different treatments trying to find out what was NOT wrong.

What David finally discerned from this meeting of the minds and wills was that no one was monitoring my overall treatment. Each physician was working independently, causing the negative interactions of various drugs. Moreover, as none of these physicians was God, as you can guess, David won the arguments. At last, everyone was now on the same page with respect to paying attention to what the others were doing rather than focusing on their personal little piece of the puzzle.

As a result, my drug regimen was changed, and my heart, although still beating faster than normal, slowed down. Then I began to stabilize. From that point forward, every healthcare worker who came within ten feet of my bedside was looking over his shoulder in fear of antagonizing the tenacious doctor whom God had sent to keep me from falling over the brink of death. However, my string of miracles was not yet over.

Miracle Number 4 – "Places Everyone" Part III

Day five in ICU was the day that had Sherry at the end of her rope. I was a bit more stable, thanks to David, but after spending another frustrating day of no answers and no clues as to what was wrong with her husband, Sherry felt that the stresses and pressures of the situation had become too great to bear. At home that evening after another tiring vigil at my bedside and on the edge of an emotional breakdown, Sherry heard the phone ring. The call was from someone who she had never met, who was calling from New Jersey of all places. This person told Sherry that a prayer chain of people in several states were all praying for God to be with her and the boys and for his healing touch on me.

For Sherry, that phone call put into perspective the wondrous power of God's unconditional love. How else could a community of his people scattered throughout the country come together to pray for someone who was unknown to them, someone they would probably never meet? This response truly embodies his command for us to "love our neighbors as we would love ourselves" (Matthew 19:19) and why Christ encourages us "to pray for others" (Matthew 5:44). Sherry could not hold her fear and pain inside any longer.

In our living room, she fell to her knees as her emotions poured out in uncontrollable tears. She later told me that at that moment she prayed harder to God than at any other time in her life. The realities of going on without her husband brought her to the universal power that is above and beyond all science and modern medicine, our creator and loving God. After praying so hard that evening, she eventually collapsed in utter exhaustion and slept the remainder of the night on the living room floor. She felt as if God was telling her to rest and trust in him. I was in his hands now; he just wanted us to **be alert!**

Arriving the next morning at the hospital, Sherry found the same set of circumstances that she had faced on days one, two, three, four, and five: no changes, no improvements and no clues, beyond a probability that I may have something called pulmonary fibrosis. But no one knew anything for sure. For five days, a steady stream of infectious disease doctors, cardiologists, neurologists, and probably even a foot doctor or two had come to examine me and then left scratching their heads. They hit dead end after dead end after dead end. Sounds like a good time for God to intervene.

At her wits end with the parade of clueless medical professionals, Sherry felt an **alerting** urge to call my best friend, Dr. David. This time, however, instead of talking to David, Sherry reached his wife, Dr. Stephanie. "Stephanie, this is Sherry. Listen, I'm sorry to have to bother you, but I'm at the end of my rope. I've lost count of the doctors and specialists that have come to see Paul. Not a single one of them has a clue as to what is wrong or how to treat him. I'm tired of dealing with these people; so I'm just going to ask you. You work with many specialists. Who is the best pulmonary doctor that you know and could recommend to me? If I have to move Paul to a different hospital to see him or her, I'll do it. I just can't take this uncertainty anymore."

Stephanie did not hesitate. "I would have Dr. Kaplan see him. I have worked with him for several years at my hospital, and in my opinion, he is the best that there is. But I don't think that he sees patients at your hospital."

Sherry thanked Stephanie for her candor and advice, pressed END on her cell phone, and walked to the ICU's nursing station to ask for a phone book to look up Dr. Kaplan's office number. Flipping through the white and yellow pages, Sherry realized that she had forgotten to ask Stephanie for the spelling of Dr. Kaplan's name, and she did not know if it was spelled with a K or a C. She asked the nurse who gave her the directory, "I'm trying to look up a pulmonary doctor by the name of Kaplan, and I'm not sure where to look: under C or K."

The nurse looked at Sherry, astonished, and pointed to a man clad in a white jacket standing about twenty feet from them. "That's Dr. Kaplan standing right there," she said.

Sherry did not hesitate for a nanosecond as she ran to Dr. Kaplan, introduced herself, dropped Dr. Stephanie's name, and asked for a minute of his time. Apparently Dr. Kaplan would on occasion work at the hospital where I was, and on that day, something compelled him to stop by the ICU to make the rounds and greet the staff, miracle number four. In their conversation, Sherry conveyed my circumstances to Dr. Kaplan, emphasizing the fact that no progress was being made with respect to my condition or diagnosis to date. "Dr. Kaplan, would it be possible for you to take a look at my husband? Stephanie said that if there was anybody to consult for a second or, in Paul's case, first opinion, you were the person."

Knowing that I was under the primary care of another physician who was also a former partner of his, Dr. Kaplan asked Sherry to follow hospital protocol and submit the request forms for him to examine me. Once that procedure was set in motion, Kaplan would wait in the ICU while the paperwork was being processed and then be more than happy to check on me and see if he could discover anything.

With the paper work done, Dr. Kaplan did come to my room later that day, begin looking over my charts, and perform an in-depth examination. About an hour had passed when he came to see Sherry in the ICU visitor's room. He began to explain his findings and his suspicions as to why I was not responding to the treatment that my other doctors were prescribing.

"Mrs. Ulasien, first of all, I am so glad that we stumbled into each other and you asked me to look at your husband. The reason I say so is that I've got an idea as to what may be going on with him and why his condition is not improving. Based on that idea, I suggest that we do a couple of things and do them quickly. Now the reasons why I suggest that we move quickly are two-fold. First, in looking at the pathology report of your husband's biopsy, I **disagree** with their findings and conclusions. I do not think that your husband has pulmonary fibrosis as described in the report, but another form of fibrosis that is less severe with a much better prognosis. Second, if my suspicions are correct, and I believe that they are, your husband is being treated with the wrong medications and will not get any better unless we change them. Right now, your husband is on a regimen of antibiotics to treat an infection that no one knows for sure if he has or not. With that uncertainty in mind, we need to add a regimen of corticosteroids to his medications to bring him around, because I am convinced that inflammation, not infection, is the root cause of his lung dysfunctions. The corticosteroids will treat the inflammation, and his lung function should improve fairly quickly.

Now before I order that medication, I would like to consult with his surgeon, Dr. Sams, about sending his biopsy samples to the pathology department at the Mayo Clinic for confirmation. If we move now, I can call ahead to Mayo and overnight your husband's samples so that they will be looking for them first thing in the morning. We may even get some feedback by tomorrow morning. If that course of action is okay with you, I've already written the orders to set things into motion. All I need is your approval." Sherry's response was only two words: "Do it!"

As Dr. Kaplan had planned, a call from the Mayo Clinic came the next day, and his suspicions were now a confirmed diagnosis. Contrary to the original pathology report, I did not have Idiopathic Pulmonary Fibrosis (IPF) with an almost zero prognosis, but a rare and treatable inflammatory disease* called Desquamative Interstitial Pneumonia (DIP) with a good prognosis. As Dr. Kaplan had suggested, once I was started on the corticosteroid, prednisone, I immediately began to respond, and my condition turned the corner. *(*Author's note: A bit of disagreement exists in the field of pulmonary medicine as to whether DIP is a category of pulmonary inflammatory disease unto itself or an early stage of IPF, hence the reference to an inflammatory disease).*

This whole chain of events was not some amazing coincidence. I am sure of that fact, as are Sherry and even Dr. Kaplan. If this intervention were the only instance of a miracle in my journey to and from the brink of death, the assumption of an amazing coincidence could have some validity. However, if you look at the succession of the previous three miracles that God gave to us, you can see a distinctive pattern emerge. In each instance, the exact right people were present in the exact right place and the exact right time. Too much precision and timeliness characterized the events to make them merely an amazing coincidence. Instead, we witnessed nothing less than the amazing grace of a string of miracles!

Miracle Number 5 - One for the family

Day six in ICU on the respirator turned into day seven and then into day eight. True to Dr. Kaplan's diagnosis and prescribed treatment, I did begin to respond and improve. Although Sherry and the boys said that I became more responsive, I was still unable to speak around the breathing tube in my throat. My only method of communication beyond acknowledging their presence was via semi-intelligible scribbling on a sheet of paper attached to a clipboard. I do not recall any of these instances except for one.

Normally, patients on a respirator receive heavy duty sedatives that not only knock them for a loop but also cause temporary amnesia in order to keep them calm. However, conscious recollections can recur for brief periods, and God decided during one of these brief conscious periods that the time had come for a miracle for the family.

You have to try to imagine the anxiety that Sherry, Matt, and Jon suffered. Only a few short days ago, the person they considered the rock of the family, the strength and stability on which they had all come to rely in good times and bad was now lying helpless and unable to provide them with what they had for years come to expect.

None of us were quite sure as to which day it was, but apparently Sherry, her father, and maybe one or both of my sons (no one can remember) were in the ICU visiting when I seemed to be partially alert and responsive to their questions. During this one instance, I distinctly remember Sherry talking to me and showing me some very gross before and after pictures of my lung that were taken during my surgery. Sherry told me what had happened and what the doctors (actually Dr. Kaplan) had concluded about my condition.

Before I continue, I need to preface a few things as well as make a few dark confessions about myself. Of the many personality traits that I possess, one can be considered redeeming and one cannot. One of my redeeming qualities is a desire to focus always on the lighter side of life, which is coupled with a tremendous sense of humor. I like to joke with people and make them smile, because laughter has always been a big part of my life and a big part of our family's life. As the late great comedian Red Skelton put it, "Why take life so seriously? You don't come out of it alive anyway!"

One of my not-so-redeeming qualities is my quick-draw wit and sharp tongue. I tend to shoot straight from the hip and not mince words while I pull the trigger. Such a response was just a way of life for a boy growing up in the old ethnic neighborhoods of my youth. Though I am not particularly proud of this habit, people have come to expect it of me. I guess that I am gingerly trying to allude to the fact that, in certain situations, I have no aversions to letting a few colorful words or metaphors fly. I have tried to change this behavior many times, but it just does not &*^$$@ing work. See what I mean?

So there Sherry, Richard and the boys were after several days filled with anxiety beyond anyone's comprehension. They were sitting and waiting for any sign I was still inside that shell of a person attached to all those machines. They were also looking for a sign that I would re-manifest myself somehow, someway. As Sherry was talking to me and showing me those gross pictures, she said, "Hon, you have something called DIP," the acronym for Desquamative Interstitial Pneumonia, "but the doctors say that you are going to be just fine." She avoided mentioning the fact I was still in ICU and that I had been there for several days. But when I heard the letters "DIP," or in my mind merely the word "dip," I began to motion with my hands for a pen to write something on the clipboard.

Sherry reached for the clipboard, put a pen into my hand, and guided it to the surface of the paper. What did I write on that sheet of paper? Hearing the word "dip," my quick-draw wit immediately thought of dip-shit; so I wrote on the sheet of paper attached to the clipboard, "SHIT." Everyone in the room began to laugh uncontrollably.

Now many of you reading this incident may be thinking to yourselves: *How can writing that particular word on a piece of paper be in any way misconstrued as a miracle from God?* In one way, you may be correct in questioning my assertions, but in another way, you might consider the circumstances. We are all familiar with the oft-used phrase, "The Lord moves in mysterious ways." Well, in his own mysterious way, through my off-colored sense of humor, he was assuring the closest of those who were hurting the most that I was indeed alive inside of the bionic man wired to all those machines. He was also assuring them through grace that somehow I would emerge again. After all, God does have a great resume' for rescuing people from the brink of death and beyond. For the Ulasien family, although in a crude and rude manner, God was saying to them that he was about to do so again.

Sherry, Richard, Matt, and Jon could have asked for no greater miracle. Kooky old Dad was still with them and would continue to be with them. God's love and his response to prayer may not always appear in the manner we perhaps have come to expect, but if we place our trust and faith in him, we know through even the most subtle and unusual ways that he is always with us.

From this point on, I began to respond more in my usual off-the-cuff manner. Even though the medical experts were not yet ready to declare that I was completely out of the woods, Sherry and everyone else knew better. I was coming back; God was not going to let me die!

Chapter 7

God's Answer to Fear

I was getting better, and my lungs were getting stronger and more able to provide my body with oxygen. Subsequently, as day ten approached, Dr. Kaplan decided to wean me off the respirator and let me start breathing on my own. Of course, in order to draw breath, I had to be more lucid. Therefore, the heavy duty regimen of narcotics keeping me immobile and quiet while I recovered had to diminish as well.

I was still unconscious or at least unaware of the point in time when the endotracheal tube from the respirator was removed and I was switched over to an oxygen mask. As the narcotic effects began to wane, I did recollect my first waking experience, and it was something I will never forget.

If you remember from the previous chapter, my last conscious memory before I faded away, not knowing if I was passing out or passing away, was flinging my arms violently, fighting for air, and thinking to myself: *Oh God, please don't let me die.* After that time, I had little to no recognition of where I was or how long I had been there. Regardless, now I was hearing a peculiarly loud hissing noise. Opening my eyes for the first time, I felt a sense of relief, thinking to myself: *I must have only passed out, because I am still alive.*

At that time, I had no idea how long I had been out. As far as I knew, it had only been an hour or two. I began to move my arms and feel around the bed to touch my face and everything else my hands could reach.

Next, I almost immediately began to sense the seriousness of where I was and the state of my condition. The loud hissing noise that I was hearing was the oxygen flowing through a small mask covering my nose and mouth. Even though I knew at that time I was alive, I also realized that I was in a state of complete helplessness and dependency.

After a few moments of waking, I was better able to focus my eyes. I looked at my hands and was shocked at what I saw. The tanned, muscular hands that I had seen and used hundreds of times a day for so many years now looked foreign. The only way that I knew they were mine was that I could somewhat command them to lift and rotate, but I thought to myself: *These hands cannot be mine.* They were yellow and puffy and had an eerie, scaly look to them. My fingernails were chalky white and had grown far beyond the length that I normally kept. I looked at my arms and saw the tubes galore coming out of them. Like my hands, my arms as well were yellow and puffy with scaly skin.

I am by nature very near sighted, and so seeing clearly beyond my arms and hands requires glasses, whether I am drugged or not. I could discern the shapes of people moving about the room and in an area directly to my right. As I looked to my left, up, and then behind me, I could see a host of machines and monitors surrounding me. Then I became frightened far beyond any other time of my life. I realized that I was in a serious situation, and I was scared, more scared than I had ever been before.

I am not a person who typically cries out in fear; in fact, I have a reputation of being somewhat fearless. Diving into open water coral reefs, driving a car at speeds of up to 150 mph, and doing loops in small airplanes are all feats that I have done for a thrill: yeehaa! In the past, I had always been in charge of my life and in control of my circumstances. Now, for the first time in my life, I realized that I had absolutely zero control and that I was at the complete mercy of God. I began to weep, and as I wept, I prayed as I have never prayed before. That prayer fervently continued the plea that I prayed ten days prior as my last conscious thought: *Oh God, please don't let me die!*

God Is Real

At the very beginning of this book, I stated that the dire set of circumstances in which I had found myself were not the result of God punishing me for anything or trying to teach me a lesson about **the balance sheet.** I was in this ICU and set of circumstances because of the poor choices I had made over a lifetime of spiritual wandering. Now that God had my undivided attention, the time had arrived for me to gain a bit of perspective.

To this day, anyone who inquires about my experiences while teetering at the brink of death almost always asks the predictable question: "Did you see a bright light?" or "Did you see **the** light?" Almost on cue, I can anticipate the disappointed expressions on their faces when I answer with a resounding, "**NO!**"

You may have just experienced a moment of disappointment as well. Believe me, everyone does. That hunger for proof is one of the frailties of faith. Those believers are few and far between who would not feel some disappointment at the lack of hard evidence that God does exist. Most of us want to believe that he is real, but many of us can also confess that we have wondered from time to time about God and heaven and whether they are fact or fiction. Perhaps that curiosity haunts us because we far too often supplant faith with a "seeing is believing" mentality. I am no different, and neither are you, because at some point of time in our lives we have all questioned God's existence. So immediately after seeing those disappointed reactions to my resounding **"NO,"** I follow my answer with, "God did not need to send me the light to prove that he was real; he just loved me enough to **show up in person!**"

Now I will admit that after I make that statement, the expressions of disappointment turn at the speed of light to perplexing blank stares, with no further questions. I make that statement not in order to suppress any further questioning but because it is the only answer I can make, because that is exactly what happened.

In my most vulnerable state of adult life when God had my undivided attention, God bestowed on me the greatest blessing that I have ever had or will ever have: the rock-solid assurance that God is indeed real and with me. This assurance is also the greatest gift of answered prayer that I could expect. As I lay in the ICU room, praying that he would not let me die, God showed up, or as I should say, he showed his presence to me.

The hissing noise of the oxygen mask continued as I wept uncontrollably. I remember reaching up with my swollen, yellow, scaly hands to wipe my tears, when suddenly a soothing substance that I can best describe as a silky, bright white shroud of many, many layers enveloped me. As I tried to touch it, it swirled around my arms and enveloped them like a mist. I kept trying to grab it and push it away, as I thought that something was hanging above my bed, but each time I reached for it, it kept swirling around my arms, staying just out of my grasp. I continued my futile attempts to tug and pull at this strange shroud swirling around me until something caused my hands to drop immediately to my sides.

We all have seen movies or heard sermons featuring the concept of the booming voice out of the wilderness or from a fiery bush as how God speaks to us. That dramatization is convenient for Hollywood, but it is a gross misrepresentation of God's true voice. This contradiction is also the hardest aspect for many who have heard his voice to describe, but through many hours of reflection and prayer, I present my humble attempt.

With my hands down to my side, I noticed the swirl of the soothing white shroud abate and become completely still. In this stillness, the telepathic sensation that I had felt prior to my surgery came to me once again, communicating: "I'm here; don't be afraid." God, the creator of all things in the universe, was revealing his presence in an obscure ICU room for Paul Ulasien from Kansas to see. I was suddenly at peace.

I'm sorry for the lack of a long dissertation about the metaphysical nature of God the creator. I do not have a plethora of scripture or text to prove the existence of God. That image of God is best left to the theologians and scholars looking for God in the terms of complexity instead of the simplicity of what I saw and how he revealed his presence to me.

At that point in my life, I was at my most compromised state since birth. Like a newborn, I was helpless, alone, and lost in unfamiliar surroundings. Likewise, as a newborn probably experiences its first sensation of fear, I was also in fear. But those lonely, fearful times are when God draws near to comfort us and to reassure us that we are never alone. I think that as newborns we probably sense this presence, but cannot remember it. Being present at the birth of both my sons, I believe that I have witnessed God's first revelation to us at birth; however, like everyone, I did not realize this grace until my reconnection to him in the ICU room.

As I said, I was blessed to be present at both my son's births. As they drew their first breaths, the shock and fear of being helpless, alone, and lost in unfamiliar surroundings undoubtedly contributed to their screams and cries for help. However, after a few moments of that uncontrollable fear, each of my boys became quiet and looked about the room in wonder and peace. Why? Even though we cannot remember this first moment of life, that same silky white shroud of many, many layers communicating the telepathic sense of "I'm here; don't be afraid" must have given us our first experience of sweet peace.

That description is God in the plainest, simplest and most straight forward terms that I can use. He is not the booming voice from the burning bush or a pillar of fire descending from the heavens, even though I do not doubt those early biblical depictions of God revealing himself, nor am I trying to contradict them. But for me and I believe for millions of others, when God speaks to us, we do not hear a voice but a telepathic sensation that even a newborn infant can understand. As a personal experience, my encounter with God is the only way that I can describe him. I believe that I did not see the light as I was teetering at the brink of death so that I could see and feel his presence instead.

God was not trying to draw me towards him; my time for crossing over had not come yet. However, God was trying to reassure me nonetheless. He was reassuring me that he was with me then as he has been with me since, as well as before my birth. When the time does come to call me home, he will still be with me as he most aptly promised through Jesus' words that "I am with you always, even to the end of the age" (Matthew 28:20).

A long period of sleep followed; however, my encounter with God was far from ended. I knew that he was keeping watch over me, but I was still seriously ill and extremely weak. Although I was no longer afraid, I was far from out of the woods, medically speaking. Faith had to take over, the faith that God was with me, the faith that if I put all things into his hands he would deliver me according to his will and his plans for my life. I could draw strength from that faith, and believe me; I needed all the strength I could get.

I learned a bit later that after only forty-eight hours of lying motionless, one's muscles will begin to atrophy or deteriorate. With forty-eight hours equal to two days and with me being in the ICU for ten days, take two and divide by ten, and that would be the state to which my physical strength had deteriorated. In terms of a percentage, that figure equates to a minimum twenty percent of my strength now gone, which in reality felt more like fifty percent.

Imagine if you will waking tomorrow morning, sitting up in bed, draping your legs over the edge of your bed, and then standing with a fifty-pound sack of sand on each shoulder. This picture is how I can best describe how far my strength had deteriorated and how extremely weak I was. Before I entered the hospital, I weighed two hundred twenty pounds and was as strong as an ox. After day eleven in ICU, I weighed approximately one hundred ninety pounds and could not lift myself to sit upright in my bed. Doing the math, I lost thirty pounds in ten days, perhaps a dream come true for someone who had always wanted to lose a few pounds here or there, but not a method I would recommend to anyone.

I was unprepared for some other surprises that greeted me as I returned to consciousness. The tremendous amount of narcotics that I absorbed while on the respirator threw my cognitive and motor functions completely out of whack. My brain seemed to be on one wave length while the rest of my body was on another.

An example of this effect occurred on my second or third day of consciousness. Sherry had brought my cell phone so that I could have a way to call her other than the hospital room phone. By using my cell phone, I could avoid long distance charges being added to my room bill, as the hospital was in another city and area code. The idea was good enough, but it turned into a huge source of frustration. I could pick up my cell phone and flip it open to talk, but I could not dial the number. Though I knew my home number and could visualize it in my head, when I sent the signals to my fingers to dial the number, my thumb would wander aimlessly across the keypad as though it wore blinders.

Simple tasks such as brushing my teeth and trying to shave ten-plus days' worth of beard from my face were equally frustrating. Shaving with a razor required the ability to negotiate the proper angle of my face versus the razor. When a nurse came to check on me, I had shaving cream all over my face, but I could not decide which end of the razor to use. Thank God the nurse interrupted me before I sliced my face to shreds.

Brushing my teeth was no less frustrating, but the nurses probably thought it was equally as comical as my attempt to shave. I was brushing everything from my neck up with a toothbrush and had toothpaste everywhere except for my mouth. When I did finally succeed in finding my mouth, I was so frustrated and exhausted that all I could do was suck what toothpaste remained off the brush.

Nothing worked, not even my cognitive recognition of such random and simple pastimes as watching sports. I am an avid football and baseball fan. Imagine my frustration when watching a sports channel highlights show on my ICU room TV where I observed people running around a field throwing, hitting, and catching a ball. I knew that this collection of activity was called baseball, but I had no idea how the game was played. The same thing happened with the football highlight films of players recently drafted into the NFL. I knew that they were playing a game called football that I had seen played thousands of times in my life, but I had a zero concept of what the athletes were doing or how the game was played.

I learned later that what I was experiencing was very similar to the symptoms of a stroke victim. The after effects of the narcotics simulated a stroke occurring. A stroke interrupts blood flow to part of the brain, and those brain cells quickly begin to die, causing paralysis, speech impairment, and loss of memory and reasoning ability. In my case, however, my brain cells were not dead, but merely numbed by more than ten days of narcotics which rendered them either unresponsive or slow to respond.

Over time, my responses did get back to normal, but the process was slow. The frustration I was experiencing spilled over into emotional outbursts that, in retrospect, I regret. I was short and abrupt with family and hospital staff, or in other words, a real grouch. Therefore, I can empathize with those who have had strokes. I experienced firsthand how damage to the brain can upset a lifetime of normalcy. One minute everything is in order, much like a completed jigsaw puzzle. Then in the blink of an eye, a crisis tosses the jigsaw puzzle into the air, and it shatters into thousands of random pieces upon landing.

Here is where faith that God was with me was so important to my survival and recovery. I cannot fathom experiencing such frustration alone and without faith. People who through some cataclysmic event only come to God out of convenience have no idea what they are missing even when life is good. Faith is such a powerful component of everyday life. Having a faith in a God who is with me always, twenty-four hours a day for three hundred sixty-five days a year for year after year, provides a comfort beyond literary description. Even in times when my faith has been challenged, God has a way of reminding me of his promise to be with me always.

Just like in the Brothers Grimm fairytale of Hansel and Gretel, who tried to leave a trail of breadcrumbs to lead them back home, God who is with us always also leaves a few reminders like breadcrumbs to infuse strength into a faltering faith. A massive faith infusion came to me on day two of consciousness.

Although I knew that God was with me, based on all the surprises I have been describing to you, my faith in what

God had in store with respect to surviving needed a bit of reinforcement. I was still praying for God to let me live, because I loved life so much; so I guess he felt he needed to drop a few breadcrumbs of faith my way.

Given my weakened state and numerous maladies, I was desperate to find something to grasp for assurance that I would indeed survive. My first faith breadcrumb began with a 10" x 12" manila envelope that came in the mail while I was unconscious in the ICU. Sherry decided to wait to deliver the envelope until she felt that I was more able to comprehend its contents. The contents of this envelope were from a publisher to which I had submitted a manuscript prior to my hospitalization. As a first time author, I struggled for several months to get a publisher just to acknowledge I existed, let alone accept my book for publication. Inside this envelope were an acceptance letter and a contract to publish my first book, *The Corporate Rat Race: The Rats Are Winning*. Because I was still a bit dingy in the head, the words on the letter would not hold still long enough for me to comprehend what they said; so Sherry read me the letter. As my jaw dropped in shock and tears of joy streamed down Sherry's cheeks, just as I had sensed God's words "I'm here; don't be afraid" a day or two earlier, I now sensed God saying to me, "You have a lot of work to do." For the first time and from that point on, I knew I was going to be all right.

I am alive, and God has dropped in my lap not only a few breadcrumbs of faith but a whole darned bakery. I was going to be all right! So now was the time to get out of bed, get dressed, and go home, right? When I felt God telling me that I had more work to do, I thought he meant only that I had a great deal of work to do before my book was ready. However, as I returned to reality, I began to realize that I had more work than I could ever imagine just getting out of the confounded hospital. Ah yes, I had a few more surprises waiting.

The endotracheal tube in my throat did keep me alive for those ten days on a respirator, but it also damaged other parts of my throat. This damage seriously compromised my ability to swallow or to keep from aspirating food into my lungs. So lucky me, I got a feeding tube. Those things are horrible, as they are inserted through the nostrils down the throat into the stomach and are left there until removed. YUCK! With this tube inside me, I could not take anything by mouth, not even a piece of ice. Therefore, even though I received fluids intravenously, I had never experienced such a desperate thirst for even a damp wash cloth. With this tube inside of my nose, not to mention all the other tubes and hoses that occupied just about every orifice of my body, getting out of bed for even a minute took a crew of two nurses and my wife to hold and maneuver all the tubes and hoses. I felt and looked like a human porcupine. Talk about total embarrassment!

As time elapsed and days passed, I did begin to shed a few of the tubes and hoses one by one, as well as my space in the ICU, which I gladly traded for a regular patient's room. Out of ICU and after about three days (the longest three days of my life), the feeding tube came out. Then a day or two later, out came the urine catheter (that hurt like the dickens), and finally I went from an oxygen mask to a more comfortable nasal cannula. I attempted to eat regular food, but I could hardly classify that stuff they gave me in the hospital as food. So I began to conspire with family and visitors to sneak me some cheeseburgers and fries from McDonalds and a nearby Sonic Drive-in.

Just as I was beginning to see some light at the end of my hospital tunnel, I woke in the middle of the night about halfway through the conscious period of my hospital stay, coughing uncontrollably. I had contracted hospital-acquired pneumonia. When Dr. Kaplan put me on the corticosteroids, the other two doctors, Dr. Howard and Dr. Fine, decided against Kaplan's advice to take me off the antibiotics: a big mistake. With my lungs in a weakened condition and my ability to breathe limited, I was a prime candidate for hospital-acquired pneumonia. This development was like taking two steps forward and one back, or in my case, maybe one and a half steps back.

Hospital-acquired pneumonia tends to be more serious, because a person's defense mechanisms against infection are often impaired during a hospital stay. Moreover, believe it or not, the types of germs present in a hospital are frequently more dangerous than those encountered in the community. With my overall health in such a tenuous position, the hospital treated my pneumonia very aggressively the moment I contracted it. This aggressive treatment entailed respiratory therapy every four hours, which consisted of breathing some disgusting, salty-tasting stuff. Nurses constantly monitored me on the hour every hour, including drawing my blood, giving me medication, and taking my temperature. This care basically left me exhausted from a near complete lack of sleep. My exhaustion became so acute that I was unable to get out of bed, not a great condition for a person who had just lost thirty pounds and part of a lung.

Dear God, I know that I have a great deal of work to do, but could you please pass me a few more breadcrumbs of faith?

Chapter 8

Time is of the Essence and the Essence of Time

The pneumonia symptoms developed suddenly and overnight. Until the medical staff diagnosed the problem, I was very restless with the cough that I had developed as well as a fever. Delirium and hallucinations are not uncommon when under the influence of a fever. Having had a few fevers over my lifetime, I can attest to my mind playing games on me under the influence of a fever, but then subsiding as the fever decreased. Another thing that I can remember about my past bouts with fever and the impact that they had on my cognitive resources is that I had no permanent recollection of the tricks that my mind played on me, just the impression that I felt a bit goofy and dreamed some weird dreams.

So along with all the other things that I had to handle, I once more slipped into a helpless and vulnerable state, a state much like my first cognizant recollections after coming off the respirator. God sure does like to arrive at these points in my life. Now while God once more had my complete and undivided attention, he and I needed to go over a few more things. This time, however, he did not want to relate his existence and presence in your lives and mine. No, this time he shared something I would need to gain and ultimately share with you: the choice of a positive perspective!

I know that this assertion sounds a bit deep, and believe me, it has been the most difficult portion of my at-the-brink experience to comprehend. Perhaps its joint importance and difficulty is also the reason why I took a six-month break from writing this book to reflect and pray about just how God wanted me to describe this message to you. Here goes.

First of all, let me reiterate that my state of pneumonia and fever did not influence what I was about to experience. The massive amounts of antibiotics that I received ridded me of the fever after only about twelve hours, when I was resting comfortably enough to fall into a few short periods of deep sleep. During these short periods of deep sleep, I began to have the most crystalline series of dreams that I have ever had. They were so crystalline that I can still recall them in detail and content as sharply now (in 2007, over two years later) as the day that I had them. Also, each of this series of dreams was interrelated. By that statement I mean that each subsequent dream directly related to the next dream and built upon the previous dream, as well as tying together all the previous dreams.

I know that this description may sound a bit queer or eccentric, and it has been a load to comprehend for me as well. Nevertheless, the lingering clarity and the succession of each dream burned so deeply into my psyche that they have given me the faith to believe that this message was not just a happenstance or a side effect of fever or drugs. No, God once again had my undivided attention, and while I was on the path he had hoped I would walk so many years ago, I was to **be alert** as He **stimulated my mind** so that I could couple my experiences with the gift of writing God gave me.

The Intrinsic Properties of Time

Time is of the essence, and the essence of time. To many of you, this statement may sound somewhat rhetorical or even a bit of an oxymoron. You may also be asking yourself: *Which is it going to be, time or essence?* In the context of how I perceived and came to comprehend these dreams, my answer to that question is not to create a distinction between time and essence, but to understand the symbiotic relationship of time and essence.

Each of my dreams, except for the last one, associated with and revolved around various periods of my life. My entire life did not flash before me; remember that these dreams occurred well after coming off the respirator and stepping away from the very brink of death. This experience was different because, although I was familiar with the places and people I saw as I moved through the periods of my life, at the same time these people were more like images and reminders of experiences rather than actual recollections. Moreover, each dream had a defined beginning and end, yet with a distinctive transition to the next dream.

If this description confuses or perplexes you a bit, how do you think I felt? I knew at the time that I was experiencing something critically important and relevant to what God wanted me to do, but what the heck was this experience about? What was God trying to tell me? More important, did everything somehow tie together?

Time is of the Essence – A Retrospect

Time is of the essence, but the essence of time needs a beginning. In the greater universal context of time, many philosophers have argued over history with respect to the beginning of time and whether time will ever end. However, in the context of our physical being, finiteness certainly does exist, as we can identify a beginning and an end or, as described in Greek, alpha and omega. Each of us has an alpha, and someday we will also have an omega. My alpha was in May of 1953, and my omega is yet to be determined.

Everyone encounters a point in his physical consciousness from which he can begin to recall his earliest memories. In studies, the average age of the earliest memory recollections is between three and four years of age. Being an average child, I can concur. Some of my first recollections occurred around the age of three, or in 1956. The reason I know so is that I do have a few recollections of my sister Reenie, who died in 1956. I can faintly remember when she was alive, and I also have some faint memories of her funeral. This conscious alpha was also when my first dream began.

You are probably thinking to yourself: *How did you know that this dream began in 1956?* Well, in the succession of the passions in my life, number one is God, number two is my wife, number three are my sons, number four is cars, and number five is sports. However, because I had no wife or sons in 1956 and probably little to no concept of God, cars and sports were very close to the head of the line. I always sat in my mother's lap in the front seat of the car and always pleaded with my father to let me stand in his lap to drive the car. Dad would at times let me do so if we were in a parking lot or a back street with no traffic.

I remember Mom and Dad always reminiscing about how whenever my father was working on his car, I as a little fellow would stand in the front seat with my hands on the steering wheel, making slobbering and spitting motor sounds. Dad would eventually have to drag me out of the car kicking and screaming so that I would go to bed. That memory is how I know my dream began in 1956. At age three, I also knew nearly every make, model, and year of car by sight. Therefore, when this dream began with the image of a 1956 Chevy Bel Air, I could not mistake when and where I was.

In addition to seeing a 1956 Chevy, I also saw some of the players from the old Kansas City Athletics baseball team who played professional baseball in Kansas City from 1955 to 1967. Mom used to tell me that baseball games ranked just ahead of Hopalong Cassidy as my favorite TV shows.

The significance of this dream was its likeness to my first childhood memories. I distinctly saw each image, the car and the players. The car looked brand new, and the players were in their prime. I saw ball players whose faces were crystal clear images, but I did not know their names. Of course, at age three I knew what a 1956 Chevy Bel Air was, but I did not know people's names outside of my immediate family. As I saw these baseball players, I knew exactly who they were, but their names did not register.

"Mr. Ulasien, MR. ULASIEN! Sorry to have to wake you, but I'm your respiratory therapist, and it's time for your medication. I'm going to put this mask over your nose and mouth; so just breathe normally."

Thank goodness that I no longer had a feeding tube while I was being treated for the hospital-acquired pneumonia. At least I could rinse that putrid-tasting stuff out of my mouth after my breathing therapy. Because this therapist came every four hours while I was in such an exhausted state, my ability to comprehend the time of day relied on which programs were on the TV in my room. Infomercials meant late night, while soap operas showed in the late morning or early afternoon and live sports indicated evening. Therefore, sleep was sleep whenever I could get it.

After I rinsed my mouth with water and took a few swigs of orange juice, I must have fallen back to sleep, because another dream came to me that started basically where the last one ended.

I was back in my youth, but this time I was a bit older and more apt to recognize things. This dream began in my old ethnic neighborhood of Strawberry Hill. Once again the people and places were very clear and distinct. Although I recollected who people were, I still could not recall their names. They were exactly as I remembered them last: same age, same dress, and same mannerisms.

I began to drift away from my old neighborhood to other areas of the town where I grew up. I remember going to the central shopping district of Minnesota Avenue and seeing the car dealerships. My father and I kept an annual ritual of hitting all the new car showrooms every fall to see the new models. In this dream, I recalled the sights and smells of new cars just as I did in those days.

I then began to see other parts of town, and I distinctly remember going by the old railroad yards. There I saw the already abandoned old passenger stations that at the time were left standing as monuments to the heyday of passenger railroads. Today, none are left standing, but I remember when I would go to visit him at work Dad telling me about them and how important they used to be to the community. In this dream, I saw these stations as they may have been in the hustle and bustle days, but then I saw them again as I last remembered them: boarded up and abandoned.

"Mr. Ulasien, MR. ULASIEN, MR. ULASIEN! I need to weigh you!"

Trying to regain my senses in the dark room, I put on my glasses, looked up at the TV, saw an infomercial on the screen, and then looked at the clock. The clock read 4:30; so I deduced that it must be 4:30 am. The person trying to wake me was a petite nurse. Now this little nurse and I never became fast friends. Her routine when she was on duty was to do my weighing ritual at the most ridiculous of times. Weighing meant getting out of bed and standing on some wobbly, cold portable scale. She never seemed to understand that I was exhausted and weak from having been awakened less than an hour before to breathe in that nasty medication. So this nurse did not get me at one of my best moments.

I barked at her, "Go away! I'm too tired; come back later!"

"Well, when do you want me to come back?" she snapped back at me.

So I retorted, "I tell you what; I'll get out of bed right now if you give me your address and phone number."

Shaking her head back and forth, she asked, "Why should I give you my address and phone number?"

Looking her dead square in the eyes, I said, "So that after I get out of here and get well, I can wake you up at four freaking thirty in the freaking morning and see how you freaking like it!" I guess I won that exchange, because she never came back. Someone else started doing my weigh-ins at 7:30 am, just before breakfast.

After losing this battle of wills, the nurse stormed out of my room, and I started flipping the channels on the TV. I was now wide awake, but I had no need for the current infomercial's latest craze in exercise wonder-machines. I still had my glasses on as I dozed off again.

Picking up where my last dream had left off, the new dream began in my ethnic neighborhood, but then it transitioned south to the suburbs where my family moved when I was nine years old. In the old Strawberry Hill neighborhoods, each block or two had its own neighborhood markets that supplied the residents with the daily staples of food and other necessities, along with gathering places such as taverns and restaurants.

In the suburbs, the homes were larger with a greater degree of space between them. Likewise, the neighborhoods sprawled to the point where you could no longer walk to the local market on the corner or in the next block. You had to get in the car and drive ten minutes or so to a mini shopping strip with a supermarket, a pharmacy, and one or two other businesses. My parents worked every day; so the neighborhood kids and I rode our bikes to these mini shopping strips for whatever reason. We used to love going to these places particularly in the summer when we were home alone. The mini shopping strips also provided us a place to meet our friends and hang out with them.

In this dream, I was in one of those shopping strips. Yet it was not any single one of those that I remembered but a combination of many of the ones within a five-minute car ride or a fifteen-to-twenty-minute bicycle ride. Here I saw people whom I knew by name and who were also friends and classmates. These people were working in the stores in this concocted shopping strip, with one strange characteristic.

They all still looked as they did when they were young, yet at the same time they seemed to have been there for thirty or forty years. I circled the block many times, moving forward in time with each circle. Circling on my bike and then later driving a car, several times I entered the store to find the same people at the same place where I last saw them, doing the same thing yet never aging. This quality disturbed me, as I was moving along in time while they were caught in some sort of time warp.

A loud crashing sound startled me and ended this dream. I reached with my hand to my bed tray for my glasses and then realized that I still had them on. I heard a great deal of chatter and scurrying outside my door, where the nurses' station also happened to be. *Do they realize that sick people are trying to sleep just across the hall?* I thought to myself. I pushed my call button, and one of the nurses came into my room a few moments later.

"What did you need?" she asked.

I pleaded, "Could you please close my door so that I can get some sleep?"

"Oh, sorry," she replied, and she closed the door.

I fell back to sleep again.

The Essence of Time – A Prospect

Leaving the days of my youth, I now moved about town as though I was on fast-forward. I also had my first experiences of night time in these dreams. As I moved through town in day and night, I caught glimpses of catastrophic events, such as the 1981 hotel skywalk collapse in Kansas City when many people were taken to the surrounding hospitals. I found myself helping in the hospitals as a volunteer and watching ambulances coming in and out, when suddenly I moved from volunteer to patient. Tubes and devices appeared in my arms and around the room. I then saw myself in a situation very similar to my present set of circumstances.

Just like I was at the time, I saw myself in a hospital room across from a nurses' station and moved from seeing an out-of-body image of me lying in the bed to occupying my own body. As I lay in the bed, time moved rapidly forward and beyond the present. I saw images of places in time periods far into the future. Hundreds and even thousands of years passed as I lay quiet. The Earth became old and worn. Vistas appeared of new worlds where civilization had expanded, and for those left here on Earth, time seemed to slip towards an unavoidable ending. The people who still occupied Earth seemed to know that the end was coming and busily prepared for that eventuality.

While time so rapidly lapsed, I remained in my bed, tied to tubes, but these tubes were not attached to machines and other medical devices. Now, all civilization and creation was tied directly to my tubes and appeared to extract their very essence from me. The nurses now seemed more like technicians whose purpose was to make sure that I stayed alive and connected, because time could not continue without the essence that flowed from my body into those tubes. If they failed to keep me alive, all time would cease.

Over two years have passed since I had these first four dreams, and as I write these recollections, they are as clear and distinct to me as though I had just awoken from them. I have never had dreams so crystalline that I can recall each part in such detail so long after the fact. For that reason, I know that these visions were not just your everyday, run-of-the-mill dreams. God spoke to me through these dreams. But what was he trying to say, and what purpose did the dreams serve?

Feeling the significance of these dreams and fearing that I may forget them, when I was eventually discharged from the hospital and strong enough to open my laptop computer, one of the first things that I did was to journal these dreams and all the details in fear of forgetting them. Since then, I have barely had to visit that journal. However, what I did need was to visit with God to try to make sense of them.

In the days after my hospital stay, I was very busy working with editors on my first book and trying to reestablish my businesses. However, I had an overwhelming urge to begin a mind map of my experiences into the formulation of another book, this book. Describing all the events leading up to my hospitalization and during it was straightforward. What was not so straightforward, however, was how these dreams tied into my experiences in the hospital. I believed that these dreams were supposed to be a huge component of this book as well as possibly the most difficult part to describe and provide with relevance. The dreams and images replayed continually in my daily thoughts for several months. I spent a great deal of time in prayer and meditation trying to understand what they meant, and I asked God a great deal of questions as well. *God, are you speaking directly to me or through me? How am I to describe what I saw and what it meant?* The answer that I received was a familiar one: "I'm here; don't be afraid."

Making a Choice

Time is of the essence, and the essence of time. If I were to combine all the dreams that I had into a movie, that sentence would be its title. Looking back to all these dreams, I noticed a few distinct similarities and points from which to draw conclusions. First of all, the dreams of my earlier years occurred in crystal clear detail as I remembered from my first memories until I moved into the future. Nothing changed from the way I remembered, as though a time machine transported me back. This immutability is the essence of time, the inherent and unchangeable nature of the past.

We have heard these clichés so many times before: "you can't change the past," "what's done is done," and so forth. Still, too many people refuse to let go of the past. Guilt, grief, loss, or other circumstances, if not compartmentalized into memories, can consume you to the point of mental and spiritual paralysis. I still have many regrets of things past that I wish I could change, but I cannot. God, however, provides us with the optimal solution to recover from our past transgressions or hurts: the state of being protected and sanctified by the favor of God's eternal love for us, more commonly known as **grace**. Grace is the great deliverance from mental and spiritual paralysis. Though time may heal all wounds, without God's grace the wound can never heal completely.

God wants us to move forward. He said so through the words of the apostle Paul, who wrote about "forgetting what lies behind and reaching forward to what lies ahead." The past is not to be relived, only remembered. Reliving your past only enslaves you to it. If you are stuck in the past, how can you ever expect to reach forward to what lies ahead?

People who are slaves to their pasts are easy to spot. Some of the telltale emotional signs are low self-esteem and the pessimism born of a sense of helplessness. Helplessness is a debilitating condition that indicates a lack of control over one's surroundings and circumstances. Ironically, helplessness is a learned condition that can evolve from early childhood.

Each person desires a feeling of mastery over his or her environment. This sense is an important foundation for emotional development. However, an accumulation of negative events occurring over time persuades many that they are the root cause of these events. Soon helplessness causes some people to react to negative events by thinking, "I'll never be any good at this," "People just don't like me," "I'm stupid," and so on.

As life progresses and events unfold, based on a preconditioning of negativity, people allow a sense of futility to become entrenched and a learned pattern of helplessness to take control. Such people will learn to become helpless. If they allow helplessness to propagate as an accepted emotional state, their anxiety and depression can sweep away any good influence, and what lies behind will overwhelm their perspective. The good news is that helplessness is learned, and what is learned can be combated or unlearned.

Psychologically, cognitive therapy, including identifying negative interpretations of events and countering the tendency to imagine the worst, is one approach which can help a person to unlearn helplessness and to reach forward by promoting learned optimism. This psychological approach to remedy learned helplessness is both effective and valuable to many. However, a pure psychological approach may lack permanence in reaching forward to learn optimism. Remember, what can be learned can also be unlearned, and optimism is no exception.

Several years ago, I received an email which stated that the solution for many of life's problems appears in the exact center or middle of the Bible. The email gave the location for that center as Psalms 118:8. Indeed, five hundred ninety-four chapters precede Psalms 118, and five hundred ninety-four chapters follow Psalms 118. And in the center of Psalms 118 is verse 8, which when paraphrased says something to the effect that "it is better to trust in God than to trust in man."

Psychology provides many beneficial solutions to help us overcome a multitude of emotional deficiencies, but as invaluable as psychology is, it does not come with a lifetime warranty. Anyone looking for a lifetime warranty can find one at the center of God's Word – and that word is grace! Psychology can us get there, but only grace will keep us there.

Many dear friends and acquaintances of mine refuse to seek God's grace to emancipate them from their pasts. I pray for them continually. However, in the scheme of life, you and I cannot intercede to seek God's grace for them; they must do so on their own. But continue to pray that one day they will seek God's grace and be free of their pasts.

Waking in the morning with a view of life as a glass half full rather than half empty is such a compellingly beautiful experience. Therefore, no matter how hard letting go or forgiving entirely may seem, having a glass-half-full perspective is possible. Just start at the center with a little bit of grace.

Resting on past laurels can also encumber your ability to reach forward to what lies ahead. Fame and fortune can lead to infamy and misfortune if you remain content to hang your hat on past accomplishments. Such complacency enslaves you as well. I think that I saw the images of sports stars of days gone by in my first dream for this very reason. How many great athletes of the past finish their careers on the ash heap of obscurity? I can guarantee you that more than a few do. Being a slave to a personification of what you were ten or twenty years ago is only reliving the past. How many comebacks have we all witnessed that have fallen into futility? I can name several, yet in every one of them the motive was the same: the inability to let go and reach forward. Time passes these people by, just as it does anyone else. Therefore, as I said in the first chapter, God has given us such a wide path to follow with a bit a wiggle room.

All of us have many things left to accomplish in our lives and many different paths to follow. Each path that we take in life has a beginning and an end. If we come to the end of a path and stay there hoping for it to extend magically, then we may be waiting for an eternity. We should be proud of what we have done in the past, but reach forward to the possibilities of what we can yet accomplish. That is where time being of the essence comes into play.

Time is of the essence. The last in these series of four dreams dealt with that message. If you recall, I saw myself transition from an observer of events to a participant in events and then finally to being the essence of future events. For this reason, time is of the essence. I believe that God was trying to give me a message consisting of two components.

First, our decisions and actions from each moment forward affect the essence of time looking back. If through God's grace we are reaching forward to what lies ahead, then we will have little to no need to forgive or regret what lies behind. With God's grace, the decisions that we make today, tomorrow, and beyond will not commit us to servicing our past; rather, we can live free and unencumbered. An example of this fruit of grace happened to me just a few short months ago.

A company which is a client of mine sent me a check in payment for some work that I had done, a check that was nearly double my original invoice. I was anxiously waiting for this check, as I needed to pay some expenses and could not afford to wait another thirty days to have it reissued. Right away, I had to make a decision. Should I cash the check as written and hope the company would not catch the error, or call their office to make them aware of the mistake and chance having to wait another thirty days? Being a recipient of many graces from God, I obviously called my client to make them aware of their mistake. Their response was to cash the check anyway, and they would adjust my next invoice accordingly.

As simple as that decision may have seemed, consider if I made the alternate decision. I may have just gotten away with the deceit and profiteered from my disgrace. However, do not forget that what comes around goes around. Somehow, someway, I would come to regret my decision. Maybe not in a month or a year, but somewhere down the line, that duplicity would come back to haunt me. Being a slave to your past paralyzes your mind and your spirit!

Eventually, my business concluded with this client; however, word of mouth spread about my integrity and honesty. As a result, today I have more business than I had ever imagined. Reaching forward to what lies ahead, thank God for his gift of grace to help us make the right decisions that matter.

The second component of time being of the essence involves the way our lives impact future generations when our lives come to an end. What I saw as my fourth dream transcended thousands of generations into the future was that the number of generations that are to follow us does not matter. That number is for God to determine. What does matter is that we make the most of the brief period in time that we occupy. I know that encouragement sounds horribly cliché, but it is so important!

Consider the state of literature and learning if William Shakespeare and Johannes Gutenberg believed that what they were doing did not matter. What about the apostles Peter and Paul? If they had lost hope and returned to their previous vocations after the crucifixion and ascension of Christ, would we even know about Christianity? Then we could consider Sir Isaac Newton, Galileo, Leonardo da Vinci, Thomas Edison, and Albert Einstein, to name just a few. Had they taken another attitude or path, what would the state of science and technology be today?

Can you see them all plugged into us and our faith, art, or science? I can. That connection is what I saw of myself in the last dream, as I was plugged into the future and the future relied on my very essence. Each and every one of us has the same potential to make a difference with respect to time and the essence of time; however, just as in the world of physics, potentiality is null and void without an action.

Successively, this collective linkage to each era, generation, and person has the potential to inspire and sustain a continuance of time and essence. As we may feel Gutenberg, Shakespeare, and Newton plugged into us, influential predecessors plugged into them as well. Someone had to inspire them. Then they inspired us, and collectively we inspire future generations. The significance of what and who inspires us, however, is not a matter of celebrity, intellect, or a myriad of other factors. Inspiration makes that difference in a person's life no matter how insignificant or inconspicuous it may seem.

I am willing to wager that you have never heard of a woman named Catherine Weinaug. Until our paths crossed several years ago, neither had I. Catherine was the elderly mother of a very dear friend of our family, Craig. In the late 1990s, she begrudgingly moved to our city at the behest of her children. Although she was quite capable of caring for herself, a few health issues were coming to light as a result of her age, and Craig wanted her nearby in the event that she would need assistance. But she came begrudgingly because of her free spirit of exploration and independence. She did not want hovering relatives to tie her down and stifle her love of life and her insatiable need for independence.

Shortly after Craig moved Catherine to Lawrence, I had the privilege of meeting her. We hit it off instantly. I learned about her travels and mission experiences, and she learned of my fascination with the cosmos and science fiction literature. We spent many an evening talking about her adventures and my thoughts on the universe, all along developing a bond of mutual interests. She gave me a copy of Stephen Hawking's *A Brief History of Time*, and Sherry and I took her on stargazing expeditions out in the country. On one of these stargazing expeditions, Catherine revealed to us that she had authored a series of Christian children's books: *Guppies,*

Galaxies, Gardens, and God; Boats, Birds, Beasts, and Believers; and Puppet Parables for Children's Church. Like the light of a million suns illuminating all at once, she inspired me!

Until that evening, I had never once pondered the possibility of writing a book. Suddenly I could not stop asking Catherine questions about writing: what inspired her, who inspired her, what it took to become a writer, and on and on. The answer to each of my questions, however, was always the same: to have the faith. The faith she meant was the faith that God had in me to write, the faith in my potential to be a writer, the faith that would sustain me when I doubted my abilities, and the faith to believe that my writing would make a difference in at least one person's life.

Catherine Weinaug was my inspiration, and faith became my guiding light. She made a great difference in my life. I hope to make a great difference in a least one other person's life, and I have faith that that person will make a difference in another person's life so that the essence of time stays plugged in to all those who will follow. Good actions and decisions or bad actions and decisions, whether to inspire someone else to make a difference or not to extend that spark, all that we do will continue except for sinking into indifference.

Indifference has many synonyms: apathy, complacency, lethargy, detachment, unconcern, and mediocrity, just to name a few. My favorite definition of indifference is just plain not caring about anyone or anything. Is that description not a serious indictment on the current state of our world? People just do not give a damn.

We are so engrossed in our own lives and all the drama that life can bring. Does any of the following strike a familiar chord? Do not take a stand or be independent. Avoid confrontation. Do not do anything that may get you noticed, because someone may disagree with you or some kook may start stalking you. What kind of a legacy are we leaving with these kinds of attitudes? The lifelines of our essence will not be able to sustain the future if we allow ourselves to fall into an abyss of indifference. We have to make a difference. The future depends on our effort, our care. Yet because of indifference, many will think that making a difference is just too hard, that they do not have enough time in the day to try, or that they will get nothing in return for the effort.

Well, inspiring the next generation is supposed to be hard. God does not promise us a smooth road, only a safe landing if we choose to follow the path he has set for us to walk. You have all the time in the world. How you choose to make the best use of time is your decision; just remember that all things are possible through God's grace. Lastly, you may get absolutely nothing in this world in return for your time and your heart, but something wonderful waits for you beyond this world.

John Lennon once wrote, "Oh boy, when you're dead, you don't take nothing with you but your soul."[2] Therefore, with respect to your soul, here is what is in store for you: **seven words.** Those seven words are God's first words that we should strive to hear as we pass from this life into eternity: "Well done, my good and faithful servant" (Matthew 25:21). I will take those seven words over any and all the possessions I can possibly accumulate in a lifetime; how about you? Remember, "You don't take nothing with you but your soul" anyway.

Time is of the essence. But the number of chances you get to make that difference and keep the essence of time flowing become fewer and fewer as each day passes. I know, because my time almost came to a close while I still had so much to do. As fate decreed, God was not ready for me; so I got a second chance. I can assure you that I wake every morning not wanting to squander it. Today may be your last, or it could even be tomorrow. The scheme of the path in life where God wants you to walk should put a sense of urgency into you. You do not have to win a Pulitzer, Oscar, or Grammy. Maybe writing a letter, making a visit, sharing a meal, or praying for another person can extend your essence into tomorrow and beyond, but you will contribute only if you choose to take advantage of the time you have left! Time **is** of the essence. So get off your backside and get with it! Time is running out, and future generations are depending on you.

Chapter 9

The Antithesis of God

"I am with you always, even to the end of the age." I experienced that promise in my first waking moment from ten days on the respirator, and at one point in time, knowingly or unknowingly, so have you. But inasmuch as God is always with us, that which is not God, the antithesis of God, is waiting to pounce out of the shadows.

My first four dreams came in succession over the period of a late night and early morning. Another dream, however, came to me one afternoon a day or two later. I was still coming to grips with all my maladies as well as the time lost while I lay incoherent on the respirator. Flashes of things I did not recall happening continued to appear through the only medium that I had available to me, the TV on the wall in front of me. About the only event of historical significance that I missed was the election of a new pope. However, I still have some bouts of amnesia with respect to events right before my hospitalization that sometimes come up to nibble on my brain.

One such instance was the 2005 Masters Golf Tournament. I watched the 2005 tournament before I went to the hospital, but I forgot all about it. Thank goodness, I was home alone with Sherry when I was watching the 2006 Masters the next year. Phil Mickelson won in 2004 and 2006. Having no recollection of the 2005 Masters and being a big fan of Mr. Mickelson, I was elated to the point of jumping up and down, pumping my fist into the air as he sank his last putt. I was so excited in part because I labored under the misconception that Phil won the Masters two years in a row.

Traditionally in the Masters, the winner of the previous year's tournament always presents the new winner with the symbolic green blazer or jacket and helps him to don it. When I saw Tiger Woods, whom I like equally, help Phil Mickelson on with his green jacket, I stood dumbfounded and wondered out loud, "What the heck is Tiger doing giving Phil this year's green jacket?" Then it hit me: *Holy cow, I totally missed last year's tournament!* Or as I was to learn a bit later, I completely forgot it.

I was in that kind of mental mode the day of my fifth and final dream. A great deal of frustration greeted me each time I watched the news or made any attempt to return to normalcy. Most of the time, my frustration exacerbated by exhaustion led me to turn down the TV's volume and take a nap. As I slept, my fifth and final dream began at the point when my last dream of a day or two ago ended.

At first I was still in the hospital bed with tubes connecting my essence to the future. Then the tubes disappeared, and I moved to a place that at first was very pleasant. I stood at the end of a driveway leading up to a large and beautiful brick ranch home situated in a densely wooded area. As I stood on the street looking first to the left and right and then straight ahead towards the house, I saw that I was in a very exclusive and affluent neighborhood. I walked towards the home, and the garage door opened. Parked inside the garage was one of the automobiles that I have coveted for many years (remember cars are in my top five passions of life), a white 1960 Cadillac Eldorado convertible with those gorgeous tail fins. Sweet and pleasant music began to play on the car's radio, and suddenly out of the corner of the garage leading into the house walked a petite and very attractive woman, dressed in a seductive dress. As trusting and faithful as Sherry and I have been to each other over our entire marriage, during this part of the dream I thought to myself: *I hope Sherry doesn't show up, she may not understand.*

As soon that thought occurred to me, things around me began to change. I looked behind me outside the garage, and the light of day began to turn into an eerie dusk. Looking back into the garage, I watched the car that just seconds earlier had me frothing at the mouth begin to fade from brilliant white to a dark color and texture akin to scratchy wool. The music turned from sweet melodies to random and hard-driving metallic sounds. The petite and attractive woman shrank in size almost to a dwarf as her seductive clothing morphed into the exact color and texture of the car. Her face was flushed and contorted, and she began to speak in tones and words that were unrecognizable, yet at the same time seemed to carry a dark meaning.

The sky outside grew progressively darker as more people identical the once attractive woman began to approach me from of the densely wooded area. They surrounded me and began to lead me outside, where the exclusive and affluent neighborhood had transformed into a long, flat landscape, absent of trees. Running parallel to the front of the house was a dusty and narrow gravel road stretching from horizon to horizon. What was transpiring around me in this dream made me increasingly apprehensive, and so I called to God to take me away from this place. At that point, I thought I would once again sense the words, "I'm here; don't be afraid," but instead I heard nothing but silence. I was all alone; God was not there.

"Hi, hon, are you okay? Jon's here to see you." Sherry and my youngest son Jon entered the room, waking me. I groggily answered, "Huh, oh hi, sweetie, hi, Jon; how did your show go the other night at the Bottleneck? I was just taking a nap. What time is it?" *Thank God, it was only a dream.*

Even though God is with us always, it was necessary for me to see and understand the things that can come between God and us. Although God's presence is constantly there, when we place other things before God, the gap between our presence and God's presence widens, and we lose our ability to connect with him. All that is not God decrees this excommunication from God's presence as a substitute for his grace. For this very reason, God tells us in his first commandment not to "have any other gods before him" (Exodus 20:3), or more simply put, to prize no other gods in place of him. In the absence of God, the antithesis of God lurks in the shadows, waiting to pounce.

I could find an endless supply of synonyms for what I mean by the antithesis of God: words such as darkness, the abyss, the chasm, the valley of shadows, hell, and so forth. They all have the same meaning: a place devoid of God. From the beginning, some type of a natural adversarial force has necessarily existed. The adversary to light is dark, the adversary to positive is negative, the adversary to good is evil, and the adversary to God is all that is not God, including all that we put before God.

If you recall, this dream began with affluence, material possessions, and beauty. As I experienced pleasure from these images, I realized that the more I coveted these things, the more my perception of them turned adversarial. It became empty and barren, with God nowhere to be found. All the pleasantries that I experienced in the beginning of the dream were but a few of the many things that people put ahead of God: possessions, power, career, drugs, and alcohol, to name just a few.

However, a line of distinction exists that we must recognize. The phrase "all things that are not God" does not necessarily define the antithesis of God. The antithesis of God can also be what priority we give these things. God has blessed my wife and me with the ability to afford a nice home, automobiles, vacations, clothing, and other possessions that many others cannot. However, we also understand and recognize from whence all these blessings emanate, God, and place our faith in him above all else.

I know many others, on the other hand, who believe that they alone can take the credit for all their accomplishments and acquisitions. I have also witnessed how their arrogance grows to consume them over time. All that they had placed before God leaves them empty and alone. They still may have all the things that they thought were more important to them than God, but after years of spiritual malnourishment, their souls slip into atrophy.

This fate is what I saw in my final dream. All that I thought was beautiful and pleasing became creatures that wanted to control and consume me. God's message through this dream from me to you is that once we allow that which is not God to consume us, we risk spiraling further away from God, eventually into oblivion.

Oblivion, a cold dark place where loneliness and fear live, is not a place that I care to consider. One of my few innate fears is deep water where I cannot see the bottom. This fear was never more pronounced than on my honeymoon with Sherry off the coast of Maui. When we were relaxing on the beach one afternoon, I decided to do a bit of snorkeling. While I was in the water, it began to rain. I was about fifty yards from shore when I heard Sherry calling to me and turned towards the beach.

"Hon, it's raining; so I'm going back to the room," she said.

"Okay," I replied, "I'm going to stay out here for a while longer." About five minutes or so of conversation followed about not staying out too long, because we had dinner reservations and so on.

During these five or so minutes, unbeknownst to me, the current was carrying me out about another twenty to thirty yards. When we finished our conversation, I waved to Sherry, replaced my goggles and snorkel, and dove back down to what I thought was still the reef. To my horror, the coral reef and bottom were gone, and all I could see was a dark blue mass of water beneath me. Still underwater and looking back towards the shore, I saw the bottom where I had been snorkeling a few moments earlier suddenly plunging straight down into darkness. As I learned later, some of the channels around and between the islands can reach depths of six thousand feet. Panicked, I swam as hard as I could for the shore in fear that the waters and darkness were about to devour me. When I did reach the shore, I threw off my snorkeling equipment and lay on the beach, panting from sheer fright.

I envision being in oblivion away from God to be a fate as real as sinking into dark blue waters. You are all alone as you sink further and further into nothingness. The further down you go, the lonelier, darker, and farther from the safety of shore it gets. That descent into annihilation overtakes us when we put other things before God. Just as in my dream, euphoria eventually changes to darkness and loneliness. Without the shining light of God's grace to guide us, we fall deeper and deeper into the darkness and away from the light of grace. Be satisfied with what you have and who you are, but never allow pride to become your god. The consequences of that choice are only darkness and despair.

Sinking into the darkness of the antithesis of God, however, is not all gloom and doom. Hope and good news still exist. No matter how far we may sink into the darkness, God's promise to "be with [us] always, even to the end of the age" follows us into the depths. All we need to do is to call to him to save us, and He will be right there to pull us back to shore. That miracle of grace and God's love for us is one hundred percent unconditional. You have no balance sheets to reconcile, no delinquent accounts to pay. Just call to him, and he will be there. As anyone who has received God's grace can attest, its positive impact on your life is beyond words. Where else can you receive unconditional love and forgiveness from what lies behind you so that you can reach forward to what lies ahead?

Why do people risk waiting to seek God's grace sometimes until the waning moments of their lives? I wish I had the answer to that question, but I do not. All I can do is to emphasize what God has put into my heart, my mind, and my hands in writing to you. Time is of the essence, and the essence of time can only be relative when we put God above all things. All things emanate from God. All things result from God's love for us. All things are possible through God.

To supplant God in favor of anything else adversely skews our ability to integrate the importance of time and the essence of time. God wants to tell each and every one of us, "Well done, my good and faithful servant." However, he also gives us the free will to decide the path we take that will ultimately determine whether we hear those words or hear only silence. He leaves the choice to us.

Chapter 10

God's Bread Crumbs of Motivation

Just before I entered the hospital, I received a phone call from a music promotional company out of Miami informing me that my son Jon's band had been selected to perform at the Independent Music World Series (IMWS) in Chicago on May 12th. Jon is a very talented musician and songwriter, but this phone call floored me. Only six out of a thousand entries won a performance slot, and much older and more experienced musicians would give their proverbial right arms for this opportunity, let alone a young artist of twenty. The venue was also an unbelievable opportunity for the fledgling music promotions and record label that Jon, Sherry, and I had started only a few months prior.

Before my surgery, which was only supposed to sideline me for three or four days, I intended to give May 12 my undivided attention after I was released from the hospital. Of course, at this point of my hospital stay, I knew that I could personally do little to nothing to support the event. Thank God for Betsy, a young lady working for our company at the time, and for Sherry, who both stepped up and filled my place.

When the dreams ended and I slowly began to improve, the IMWS show began to occupy the forefront of my thoughts. I still believed that I needed to participate in any way that I could. During my time in ICU, Sherry received parcels in the mail containing the promotional material, including several color posters, which we needed to publicize the show on our end. Knowing how much this show meant to me and how badly I wanted to participate in it, Sherry brought one of the posters to my room and taped it to the wall in front of me, facing me every waking moment of the day. The time had come for a few more breadcrumbs from God's bakery of faith!

The sight of that poster facing me every second of the day gave me a reason to stop complaining about how exhausted or weak I felt. It acted as a constant reminder that I had a ton of work to do if I was to get out of this place and make the trip to Chicago to witness my son's big moment. As hard as the recovery was, I had to push myself beyond what I thought was possible to achieve goals such as getting out of bed, sitting in a chair, and working with the nurses to get an extension on my nasal cannula long enough to reach into the bathroom so that I could wash my hair, brush my teeth, shave, and attend to other matters of personal hygiene. I ceased moaning and groaning to the physical therapists when they came to work with me so that my atrophied muscles would start to come alive. Each time the nurses or therapists asked about my sudden change in attitude, I would point to the poster on the wall in front of me and say, "I have a lot of work to do if I'm going to make that show!"

Naturally, this change in attitude also positively impacted my recovery from hospital-acquired pneumonia. The coughing became less pronounced, and my daily x-rays showed that my lungs were clearing. A bit of light shone at the end of the tunnel, but I had to prove that I was strong enough to go home.

The challenge that the doctors set me felt like a marathon. When I was able to walk with the aid of a walker down the hall from the nurses' station and back, around fifty feet, they would consider sending me home to continue convalescing.

I love challenges; so when the doctors threw down the gauntlet of walking fifty feet, I was determined to do even more. The preparation took a bit of planning with the nurses, but I arranged for a walker to be brought to my room as well as a portable bottle of oxygen. The plan was that I would walk only with the assistance of the walker while a nurse paced me wheeling the oxygen bottle. Ironically, I planned to attempt my great feat on Sunday afternoon, the Sabbath, a day of rest but also a day of sheer determination.

Everything was in place; the nurse brought the walker to the side of my bed, switched my nasal cannula to the portable oxygen bottle, and literally hit the gas! As I slid my legs over the side of the bed and maneuvered towards the walker, the virtual fifty-pound sacks of sand still weighed on each shoulder, but this time I said to myself: *You've carried fifty-pound sacks of sand on your shoulders before. So suck it up, and start walking!*

Walking towards the door, I had to pass the poster of the IMWS show that was now only eleven days away. I looked at the poster and then turned towards the doorway, nurse and oxygen bottle in tow. Exiting the room, I made a left turn and started my trek down the hall. This hallway was a dead-end, so after what seemed to be hours, I finally reached the halfway point of my excursion, did an about face, and started to walk back towards my room. Focusing on the floor to keep my center of balance in perspective, I did not notice that my sister Rosie, my niece Georgia, her husband Dan, and their three boys were standing just to the left of the nurses' station watching. Having completed my fifty-foot hike, I was about to make a right turn back into my room when I heard someone say, "Hi Uncle Paul!" I looked up from the floor and saw my family with half smiling/half panicked looks on their faces, not knowing what to make of my little excursion. Not missing a beat, I reassuringly smiled back at them, did an about face, danced a little jig, and headed down the hall and back two more times! After three laps, I did retire to my room. As I passed the poster once more, I stopped and gave thanks to God for giving me the courage to summon what little strength I had to accomplish this simple task so that I could finally go home.

Monday morning came and, as promised, I was told that today was the day I was going to be released. After twenty days of fighting for my life, overcoming setbacks, and experiencing miracles and God's grace, I was ready to go home, almost. I was still not a well person. My doctors, however, were becoming convinced that my chances for recovery were better at home under the care of visiting nurses. The hospital-acquired pneumonia still threatened my life, and I needed to remain on the regimen of super-antibiotics that I was receiving in the hospital. Before I was allowed to leave, I needed to have a peripherally inserted central catheter, or PICC line, embedded in a vein in my arm.

A PICC line is generally inserted into one of the veins in the upper arm and then advanced with the aid of a fluoroscope towards the heart until it reaches the very tip of the heart. I had to wait six hours from the time I was told that I could go home until I was wheeled into radiology for the PICC procedure. The doctor informed me that this procedure was very uncomfortable, hospital lingo for the fact that it hurt like the dickens, but if it allowed me to get out of the hospital, my attitude was, "Bring it on!"

During the six hour wait, Sherry and I also had to make arrangements for visiting nurses to come to our house. We also needed to have an oxygen pump delivered, as well as all my intravenous meds. These items were my lifeline to recovery, and we had to assure their delivery before I left the hospital. I wish that I had written down her name, because the coordinator who worked with all the vendors and agencies to complete the arrangements was a godsend. Before I got into the chair to be wheeled out to Sherry's waiting car, this young lady attended to every detail so meticulously that all Sherry and I needed to do was drive home. I wish that I could thank her.

With the PICC line now installed, I returned to my room, dressed, and waited for the attendant with a wheelchair to start me on my way out the door to go home, a place that I had not seen for almost a month, the longest amount of time that I had ever been away! Someone that I had not seen for the same period was my constant companion for over thirteen years, our Lab-mixed dog: my Katie girl. Hardly a minute had passed while I was in the hospital that I did not think about my Katie girl, and I asked Sherry about her every day. I anticipated a joyous reunion when I walked through the front door of my home and saw my Katie girl. These thoughts and feelings filled my mind and heart as the attendant wheeled me to the hospital entrance, where I waited for Sherry to arrive, load me up, and head for home.

Sherry faced a bit of a challenge in getting me, carrying two fifty-pound sacks of sand and the oxygen bottle, all in the front of our Monte Carlo, but after a bit of maneuvering, the attendant bid us good luck, closed the car door, and watched us drive away. I looked back at the hospital as we pulled onto the boulevard and told Sherry, "I never want to see that place again!"

"Neither do I," she replied, and we drove towards home.

After all the waiting and stress of having the PICC line inserted, I was obviously tired; so I closed my eyes as we drove west on the Kansas Turnpike. I love my wife with all my heart, but she loves to talk, sometimes at the most inopportune times. However, Sherry must have sensed that I wanted to rest. Saying nothing, she quietly put a CD into the car stereo and turned down the volume. Sweet music wafted from the speakers as we drove towards Lawrence. At first I did not recognize it, but then it came to me. It was my son Jon on the piano and his friend Robert on cello playing some classical melodies that they had written just a few months earlier and recently recorded. Tears began to stream down my cheeks as I listened to the beautiful melodies. I prayed silently: *Thank you, Lord, for allowing me to hear music again, and for delivering me out of the hospital.*

After being away for such an extended period, I was dumbfounded by changes to my once-familiar environment. As we exited the turnpike and drove onto the streets of Lawrence, many things looked strange and out of place. Sixth Street, the main east/west artery through north Lawrence that we frequently drive, did not look as I had last seen it just twenty days ago. It was now a huge construction zone cluttered with orange barrels and detours. Construction closed our usual route through the neighborhood as well. We had to swing several blocks south and circle back north to get home. Even the neighborhood looked different. A late frost in 2005 had kept the grass brown when I went into the hospital, and the trees had no leaves on them. Now everything was green and in full blossom.

Our house, just a block away, had never looked as good to me as it did at that moment. During my last few days in the hospital, I had cringed at the thought of seeing my lawn with nearly a month's worth of growth. But thanks to my brother-in-law and sister-in-law, Ron and Linda, and my two sons, the manicured yard looked great.

We pulled into the driveway and parked. Sherry and I had decided to enter through the front door rather than the garage, as it had fewer steps. Steps! Oh my God, I had not thought about climbing steps. Even though I had only four steps to climb which were stretched over twenty feet of walkway, I began to feel anxious.

Sherry exited her side of the car, walked to the trunk to remove the walker, and then came back around to my side of the car. Opening the door, she maneuvered the walker so that I could stand, grabbed my arm, and helped me and my two virtual fifty-pound sacks of sand out of her Monte Carlo. With my oxygen bottle in tow, I started walking ever so slowly towards the first step. I panicked. I started to become short of breath, and I could feel my bladder about to go. Fortunately, a two-foot-high retaining wall borders our walk; so I spun around and sat on the wall.

"What's the matter, hon; are you okay?" Sherry asked frantically.

"Just give me a second to catch my breath. Just a second and I'll be all right," I replied. *God, what is wrong with me? Did I make a mistake coming home so soon?* I wondered. Once again I felt him answer, "I'm here; don't be afraid." So I cranked up the volume on my oxygen bottle to maximum flow, stood again with my fifty-pound sacks of sand on each shoulder, and placed my right foot on top of the first step. I groaned noticeably as I pushed downward with all my strength to lift my body onto the first step. I reached step number two, lifted my right foot, pushed down with all my might, groaned loudly, and continued to step number three.

"Hon, do you want to stop and rest?" Sherry asked.

"No," I replied, "just go and open the front door; I'll make it." *I'm here; don't be afraid.* The door swung open, and waiting there, wagging her tail and jumping for joy, was my Katie girl. *Thank you, Lord, for bringing me home!*

As I lay on the couch with my Katie girl at my side, I began to reflect on all that had transpired since the last time I had occupied this very same spot. *My God, I can't believe what has happened to me,* I thought to myself. *Was it just a bad dream?* The ringing of the doorbell snapped me back to reality. Ding-dong - the oxygen supply company delivered my oxygen pump and spare O^2 bottles. Ding-dong - the medical courier brought all my intravenous pumps, supplies, and medications. Ding-dong - the visiting nurses coordinator arrived to take inventory of all my necessary supplies and equipment. *No, I guess it's not a dream after all. I am so tired; I need to sleep.* Mercifully, everyone left, and I fell asleep on the couch.

Later that night, Sherry helped me to maneuver my myriad of pumps and oxygen tubes, undress, and get into our bed. For the first time in almost a month, I stretched out on my side of our bed, put my head on my own pillows, and slept.

Chapter 11

Molehills that become Mountains

We never miss something that we once took for granted until it suddenly disappears. Then and only then does our razor-sharp focus begin to notice each and every aspect of what was once simple or mundane. Molehills are rarely noticeable unless you happen to step on one. You can feel the ground give a bit as your foot compresses the soil of the tiny tunnel the mole dug, but then you move forward and forget all about it. However, if all the little molehills in your yard suddenly become snow-capped mountains, then you will definitely notice them. And you cannot just step over a mountain. To get past it, you must find the best and safest route to the top and then over the mountain. As any expert mountain climber can attest, scaling a mountain and surviving to climb another is not a haphazard occupation. He must enact an action plan with a series of many intermediate goals before he can achieve the ultimate goal of standing at the top. What can be even more daunting is having several molehills become mountains, each requiring a separate set of goals to reach their tops.

I needed to scale a giant mountain at the center of a range of smaller mountains in order to reach my ultimate goal. That giant mountain was a complete recovery and a return to normalcy. When God told me in the hospital that I had a great deal of work to do, little did I know at that time that God was preparing me for the struggles and challenges yet to come: all the little molehills that had now grown into mountains.

Mt. Standing on my Own Two Feet

Beep, beep; beep, beep. I opened my eyes, and the light in the room indicated morning. As the prescription sleep aid that the doctor had provided as part of my drug regimen was wearing off, a strange beeping noise greeted me. Looking up towards the head of the bed, I saw a red light flashing and then once again heard the beeping noise. The portable intravenous pump that was pushing antibiotics into me beeped to signal that it was running dry. Looking out of the window just to my right, I could see that daybreak had begun; so it must be time to get up. Sherry was already up, and I could hear her busily working in the kitchen.

"Sherry, could you help me get untangled from all of these tubes so that I can get up?" I called. My two IV lines and my oxygen hose had become tangled during the night.

Sherry helped me to untangle my connections and brought me my walker so that I could go to the restroom and then into the living room, where she would serve my breakfast. I felt and walked like an elderly man using a walker to get around my own house. I did not like the contraption at all; so I made up my mind that this walker was going to be the first thing I was going to eliminate.

I had to leave the walker outside the bathroom, because there was no room for it in the commode room; plus I was able to maneuver myself fairly well without it. When I exited the bathroom, I pushed the walker to my right towards the dining room. That time was the last I ever touched it. With my two fifty-pound sacks of sand and the intravenous pump around my neck, I took about twenty little old man steps towards the couch. Trying not to trip over the fifty feet of tubing connecting me to the oxygen pump, I spun around and sat down. *Bye-bye walker!* This maneuver thoroughly exhausted me; so I lay still for a while, sucking as much oxygen as I could from the cannula as I waited for breakfast.

My mother always taught me to keep busy. She espoused the philosophy that, if you do something to keep your mind off whatever is bothering you, it will pass before you know it. Mom was a very wise lady. I knew that I needed to get busy to get my mind off the intravenous contraptions hooked into me. I needed to get busy so that I would stop thinking about the fifty feet of plastic tubing lying on the floor that was still hooked to the oxygen pump I needed in order to breathe, and I needed to get busy so I could stop worrying about the hospital-acquired pneumonia.

I had just spent ten miserable conscious days lying in a hospital bed with nothing to do but watch TV, and I was not about to repeat the inaction at home. To me, watching TV was not getting busy.

"Sherry, could you do me a favor?" I asked.

"Sure; what is it?" she inquired.

"Could you bring my laptop downstairs along with the power supply? I'd like to check my emails plus maybe do a little surfing on the Internet." We have a high-speed wireless network that grants us access to email and the Internet from any room in our home. I truly missed this luxury while I was in the hospital.

I do enjoy watching a bit of TV, especially sports and old movies. However, after about ten days of doing nothing else, I could not stand the thought of spending my time convalescing at home just channel surfing. Somehow, as best as I could, I needed to get back into the swing of things, and I am glad that I did.

For anyone who relies on email as part of a daily routine, whether for work or personal reasons, an absence of almost a month can result in hundreds of unanswered emails, not including the spam. In my case, that backlog was just what the doctor, Dr. Mom, would have ordered. The many emails that I was reading took my mind off the fact that I was still attached to a number of machines and other devices. Time passed quickly that first morning, and I began to feel a bit useful.

Sitting on the couch and reading emails may have been a good bit of therapy for my mind, but something kept reminding me that if I was ever to reach my ultimate goal of complete recovery and normalcy, I needed to get off my posterior as well. Then I came back to the reality of my circumstances. In spite of the fact that I was mentally able to refocus my thoughts, the fact of the matter was that I was indeed lying on the couch sucking oxygen through a tube.

These returns to reality were huge downers. I would begin to lament about the possibility that I had reached the end of the road. I was going to be hooked to this bloody oxygen pump for the rest of my life or what was left of it. Once again, the fear of dying gripped me, and I began to cry to God.

My prayer was a familiar one: *Dear God, please don't let me die.* However, what I felt God saying back to me was not the same. I did not feel God saying to me: *I'm here; don't be afraid.* No, this time I could feel him yelling at me: S*top whimpering and get up!* I was just like the faithful brother with an abscessed tooth whose story I told several chapters ago. Just as God yelled to the brother to go see a dentist if he wanted his tooth to get better, now he yelled at me that he was not going to lift me off my couch and levitate me across the room. I was going to have to stand on my own two feet and do that on my own.

Sherry had left to run a few errands and, I think, just to get away for a bit of fresh air as well. So I did not have anyone to help me maneuver all my tubes and hoses if I needed to stand up. The prospect of jockeying a fifty-pound sack of sand on each shoulder, a portable intravenous pump in a carrying case draped around my neck, and fifty feet of plastic tubing coiled on the floor connecting me to the oxygen pump in the corner of the room was the least of my worries. Somehow I also needed to summon the strength and courage to stand and then to start walking.

As I sat on the edge of the couch with my feet on the floor, I began to think to myself: *Okay, once I stand up, then what?* I never imagined that such a simple act as standing and walking would require a plan of action. Once I was on my feet, I needed to decide where I was going to go and how far I would try to walk. That morning, I decided to walk into the kitchen, do an about-face, walk back into the living room past the couch into the bedroom, do another about-face, walk back into the living room, and then sit down. I estimated that my proposed route would cover a total distance of about fifty feet, one third of what I walked on my penultimate day in the hospital. However, I was going to take this short jaunt without the aid of a nurse and a walker.

Before I started, I murmured softly: *Dear God, please give me the courage and strength to do this.* With all my might, I simultaneously pushed down with my hands and my legs and slowly stood up. I stood still at the edge of the couch for a few moments to collect my thoughts and to make sure that I was not going to become dizzy. The last thing I wanted Sherry to see when she returned home was me unconscious or kaput in the middle of the living room, especially after I put her through so much worry in the hospital. When I felt I was all right, I slowly began to follow my predetermined route through the house. Though I took several minutes to accomplish what a couple of months ago would only take a few seconds, I reached my goal.

Exhausted, I sat back on the couch, not to relish the fact that I had just walked fifty feet on my own but to plan my next move. I began to refer to the distance that I walked that morning as one lap through the house. That afternoon, I planned to do one lap and a half, following my original route but walking past the couch a second time, going back into the kitchen, and doing an about face back into the living room before sitting down.

For the first week I was at home, each subsequent morning and afternoon I extended my walk by half a lap to the point that I was walking several hundred feet twice a day, then three times a day, four times a day, and so on. I was pushing myself a bit too hard, as my friend and life saver Dr. David would lament, but I believed that hard work was my only option. I would be forced to deal with a whole slew of mountains over the next few weeks, and pushing my strength to the edge was the only way I could meet the challenge. Besides, I was not alone. God was there to catch me in case I fell.

Disappointment Ridge

In any sport or physical activity, a wide chasm exists between the skill of a novice and that of an expert. The novice can only breach that chasm through a combination of desire and continuous improvement. Drive and determination hold little value unless you are willing to devote time to practice, and vice versa. If your heart is not in your endeavor, you will not spend the time necessary for conditioning and practice.

Again, mountaineering is an excellent example of this truth. In my younger days, I did try a bit of mountain climbing in the Alps and Rockies as a recreational activity. I loved the exhilaration and vistas that were part of climbing, but I realized that I did not have the physical ability or desire to accomplish more than what many consider to be a strenuous hike. So I would not scale Mt. Everest in my life; I just did not have the requisite desire.

Those who have successfully scaled the heights of Mt. Everest have ascended many peaks in between their first climb and their ultimate goal of the world's tallest peak. They suffered more than a few setbacks and disappointments as well. But they crossed the point of demarcation between individuals who reach the summit of a mountain and those who only think about it or make meager attempts. That point of demarcation is a concoction of one part desire and one part dctcrmination blcndcd wcll with two parts faith, known better as **courage.**

Courage is a trait that I inherited from my parents. If you recall, their whole lives traversed a strenuous series of peaks and valleys through which only courage and perseverance kept them going. Their faith and sheer determination have always inspired me, and I once more would require healthy doses of them.

Slowly but surely, I was gaining strength and becoming more able to take care of myself. I still needed Sherry's assistance to change the IV bags full of medications as well as to flush the PICC lines before and after each change of an IV bag. However, I started doing most other things on my own. In addition to Sherry and the visiting nurses, I also saw a physical therapist that came each day to help me get my atrophied muscles awake and active. I was working myself hard, probably harder than I should to make as much progress as possible, because May 12 was fast approaching. Everyone was trying to help me reach my goal of traveling to Chicago for my son's performance at the IMWS.

In the background, Sherry was hurriedly finalizing the arrangements necessary so that I could make the trip. She had arranged for an ample supply of oxygen bottles, a wheelchair, and a handicap-equipped room at the hotel in Chicago. I would not be able to fly to Chicago because of my need for oxygen; so my brother-in-law, Ron, who was also ferrying up most of the band's equipment, was going to chauffeur me.

Two days before we were to leave, I was supposed to have the PICC line removed; so Sherry made all the appointments. Her father Richard picked me up and took me to the doctor for the procedure of the PICC line removal. I was still too weak to do much walking; so with Richard's assistance, I rode in a wheelchair fitted with a portable oxygen bottle to the car and then into the doctor's office. At this time, I began to realize that I needed to come to grips with a major decision.

The entire process of getting in and out of a car with a wheelchair was more strenuous than I anticipated. Returning home from the doctor's office, I began to realize that what I had just endured was nothing compared to the ten-hour drive to and then from Chicago. I knew that I should not even consider making this trip, but then again, how could I not go? Sherry had made the arrangements, and everyone was pulling for me. Jon was also depending on his father to be there, but my body was telling me otherwise.

That evening, everyone was scurrying about the house in anticipation of the trip. Jon was downstairs with the band polishing up their set, and Sherry was busy getting things together. During a moment of brief silence, I called to Sherry to come sit with me on the couch, because I needed to talk to her. My voice cracked as I looked at Sherry and said, "Sweetie, I can't make the trip. I'm just too weak and too sick to go."

"Are you sure, hon?" she asked.

Tears began to well in my eyes as I could only shake my head in acknowledgement. After all the plans and hard work that Sherry had put into getting me to Chicago and back, I anticipated that she would be upset and possibly even angry with me. After more than twenty years of marriage, I should have known better.

"Well, I guess I'll need to cancel my reservations to stay home with you," she said. "What are we going to tell Jon and the rest of the band? They depend on you so much and want you to be there."

I told Sherry, "We need to tell them the truth; I can't make it. But you are going to have to make the trip regardless. I have already taken care of the show details with the promoter. There's a contingent of about twenty family and friends making the trip; so everything will be just fine. Jon needs one of us there, and tag, you are it!"

"What about you?" Sherry worried. "Who is going to take care of you?"

"I'll be just fine," I answered. "David is just five minutes away and can be here in a flash if I need him. I have plenty of food that I can nuke in the microwave. Besides, you are only going to be gone one night; so just go."

It was a huge disappointment to everyone that I was not going to make the trip, but it also turned out to be a huge godsend. Most venues that host live music are places where people not only congregate to listen to music but also consume adult beverages and smoke. Many municipalities ban smoking in public places, but at that time, Chicago was not one of them. The night of the performance, Sherry called me on her cell phone so that I could hear the show, but she also reported to me that the air was filled with so much smoke that my lungs could not possibly have survived. The concert may have thrown me right back into the hospital.

If we look hard enough past disappointment, we may see the glowing ember of a blessing. The courage that God gave me to face my mountain of disappointment was in actuality an Everest of a blessing in disguise.

Fifteen Stairs Peak

With only one day to go before everyone would leave for Chicago, I felt the need to do something radical to prove that I would be able to fend for myself. Every day as I did my laps with a portable IV pump and oxygen tubing in tow, each lap took me past the stairway which leads to the second floor of our home. The second floor of our home is also the location of my sanctuary from the world, my office.

In one of the daily routines of exercises that the physical therapist had prescribed, I stood at the bottom of the stairs, and using the stairway handrail, pulled myself up and then stepped back down from the first step on the stairway. She suggested that I increase the number of step-up-and-then-step-down exercises by one repetition each time. I was to continue increasing until I could do as many repetitions as there were steps on the stairway: fifteen. I am not sure if she was subliminally trying to get me to set a goal of getting to the top of the stairs or if fifteen was just an arbitrary number. To me, her reason did not make any difference. From the first lap that I took on day one, I had already determined to get to the top of those stairs as soon as I could push myself to do so.

All the disappointment of not being able to go to Chicago had subsided. I heard Sherry talking on the phone upstairs in her home office, which was cattycorner from mine, as I began my morning laps. My fifty-pound sacks of sand had lost a bit of their volume on successive days as I felt the strength slowly returning to my legs. I had also stopped counting laps as a result of my speed and endurance beginning to increase. In lieu of tracking how far I was walking in laps, I began to measure how long I was walking in time. However, regardless of time or laps, each time I walked past the bottom of the stairs, I looked up and began the process of summoning the courage to stop walking back and forth and to start walking up.

I was no fool; I knew that getting from ground level up fifteen stairs was going to be a huge undertaking. First of all,

I had to untangle all the oxygen tubing and then coil it just right so that it would not snag as I mounted the steps. I needed oxygen, and plenty of it, to get to the top. Second, I had to plan for the contingency that I might become light headed or faint. Passing out and rolling down the stairs, carpeted or not, would more than likely put me back in the hospital, if not the morgue. Last of all, I needed a few breadcrumbs of faith and a whole bowl full of Ulasien courage.

I proceeded very deliberately with my preparations that morning. As I executed my plan to get to the top of the stairs and into my office, I also needed to be very careful not to rouse Sherry, who would probably panic if she saw me trying to climb the stairs.

First things first, I needed plenty of oxygen. Since the first day of my homecoming, monitoring my blood oxygen levels with a device called a pulse-oximeter had become very important. This tiny little device fits over the end of the index finger to indicate the level of oxygen in my blood on a scale from one to one hundred. An average person would need a minimum reading of ninety to avoid becoming lightheaded and possibly fainting. If I was sedentary, my oxygen levels stayed in the ninety-one to ninety-three range even without my nasal cannula, but standing or walking or both would tank me into the mid-eighties. Therefore, in order to walk, I needed to crank up the volume on the oxygen pump to deliver more oxygen. With that requirement in mind, before I started towards the stairs I stopped by the oxygen pump and cranked that sucker up so high I thought it was going to blow my eyeballs out.

Next, with hurricane-force winds of oxygen howling into my nostrils, I gathered the fifty feet of tubing connecting my nasal cannula to the pump. At times, this tubing could be a major pain in the backside as it snagged on something, causing a whiplash effect which snapped my head backwards if I was moving too fast.

Our dog Katie was also a hazard around this tubing. With Katie's eyesight not being what it used to be, at times she did not see the tubing lying on the floor and tripped over it, disconnecting me from my supply of oxygen. Also on one occasion a few days earlier, I felt unusually dizzy after waking from a nap. I checked my blood oxygen level with the pulse oximeter, and the reading was in the mid-eighties. Needing more oxygen, I slowly made my way into the living room, where the oxygen pump was, only to find Katie sound asleep on the tubing, pinching it off. I yelled at her to get up, obviously scaring her. From that point until the pump was taken away, she tucked her tail between her legs anytime she caught sight of that tubing. So before I started to climb the stairs, I made sure that Katie was in the bedroom with the door closed so that she would not trip over the tubing or fall asleep on it.

Climb the first step; it's no problem. I had danced up and down the first step of our staircase many times the past few days as part of my therapy. The real challenge was going to be step number two. Before I attempted step number two, I once more reviewed my plan in the event I was to become faint so that I would avoid falling. After each step I took, I would stop for a few moments to make sure that I was stable and not dizzy. If I indeed felt dizzy or faint, I was going to sit immediately on whatever step I had reached and stay there until I felt able to continue or retreat.

Okay God, here I go; don't let me fall, I prayed. Then with the same motion as the first step, I pulled with my arms and pushed up with my legs to step number two. Standing on step number two, I began thinking to myself: *What did the nurses in the hospital tell me to do? Oh yeah, I should breathe in through the nose and out through the mouth. Is the room spinning? No. I guess that's a good sign. I think I'll just stand here and collect my thoughts for a minute. All right, Ulasien, let's go.* I repeated this scenario in one form or another thirteen more times until I was standing at the top of the stairway.

Before I became ill, I took just two or three seconds to get from the bottom to the top of our stairs. On this day, the ascent took twelve minutes, but by the grace of God, I made it! Even though I took my time going up the stairs, when I finally reached the top, my legs felt like rubber. Directly to the left of the top of the stairs is the doorway to my office. Making sure that I had plenty of slack in my oxygen tubing, I gingerly walked another ten or twelve steps to my office chair and collapsed into it.

"Sweetie, would you come here a second?" I called in a restrained voice, not wanting to spoil the surprise that I was only twenty or so feet from her office. "Sure," she answered. "I'll be right there; just let me finish this email."

Rounding the corner from her office and then peering towards the unanticipated sight sitting before her, Sherry stopped dead in her tracks. "OH MY GOD! HOW DID YOU GET UP HERE?" Sherry exclaimed as she cupped her hands over her mouth in astonishment.

"The only way I know how, sweetie: I walked," I said.

Whenever my wife tries to get either the dog's, Jon's, Matt's, or my attention or hollers at us in disgust, she always starts by reciting our full names, "PAUL ULASIEN, are you out of your mind?" she scolded.

"Maybe," I replied, "but I've got to get up here sooner or later. I just had a feeling I should do it now; so here I am."

I stayed in my office for about forty-five minutes checking email accounts on another home computer before I began to tire and needed to lie down. Even though going down the stairs is less strenuous than going up, someone in my condition finds that task no less stressful. Walking slowly, I took only about two minutes to descend. When I reached the bottom of the stairs, standing on terra firma, I once again thanked God and then laid down to rest.

I can honestly say that those fifteen stairs were the most meaningful climb of my life. After I scaled Fifteen Stairs Peak, other tasks such as walking to the front porch to water my flowers or just sitting in a chair outside to read the paper were now attainable, though still difficult. Eventually the sacks of sand began to lighten as I methodically regained a piece of freedom each subsequent day. My climbing Fifteen Stairs Peak also gave Sherry, Matt, and Jon the peace of mind to go to Chicago without me. I was able to start taking care of myself again.

Humility Heights

My parents set the example of living by the golden rule of treating others as you would like to be treated for my sisters and me to follow. Rarely a week passed when my parents did not invite someone down on his or her luck or just lonely to come to our house for dinner. Likewise, Mom or Dad expected us to accompany them when they visited friends or relatives who were shut-ins to bring some food or just sit and visit. I remember Mom and Dad responding to our moans and groans about having to go and visit some old person instead of staying home and playing with our friends by saying, in their badly broken English, "Don't forget; someday you may need somebody to help you."

Treating others the same way we would like to be treated has also been a way of life in my adult household, a value that Sherry and I have instilled into our sons. Whenever a friend needs a meal or a favor, my wife is always the first to step forward. Our family also tries to volunteer together a few times a year at the local outreach kitchen, the Lawrence Interdenominational Nutrition Kitchen or L.I.N.K., to cook or serve those who are in need. We look forward to each time we are able to participate as one of our favorite family times together. Whenever I contemplate going with Sherry and the boys to serve at L.I.N.K. or to help in some other capacity, I find myself thinking about all the reasons why I should not help. But then I can hear the distant echo of Mom and Dad's words, "Don't forget, someday you may need somebody to help you."

I have always been very comfortable giving to my family, friends, and others in need. Receiving, on the other hand, makes me very uncomfortable. I guess that the ideal of self-sufficiency that I imbibed in childhood has always led me to believe that I would always be able to take care of my own needs without the assistance of others. Whenever times were bad or I was down on my luck, this self-sufficiency caused me to get very stubborn and spurn the assistance of others. I just set my jaw, squared my shoulders, and marched forward.

On the outside, I was determined to prove to the world that I could indeed take care of myself while Sherry was in

Chicago. However, what no one saw inside my self-sufficient persona was the sheer terror that my stubbornness was going to land me in deep trouble. Too many things could go wrong while I was alone, and I was letting my foolish pride get in the way.

The IMWS show started at 8:00 pm on Thursday night. Everyone had taken an early morning flight to Chicago in order to check into the hotel and then have a bit of time to relax. Ron had left the day before with the band's equipment and would meet them all that afternoon. I kept up to date via cell phone on everyone's progress, an activity which also kept my mind off my impending predicament. As late afternoon approached, random thoughts began to swirl inside my head. *What if I fall while walking to the kitchen? What if the microwave doesn't work? Can I walk outside to feed or check on our cat? Can I get to the door to let Katie out? What am I going to do without Sherry?*

As the anxiety was ratcheting up to a fever pitch inside me, I heard the doorbell ring. During the daytime I usually left the front door unlocked in case I could not get to the door in time to answer someone ringing the doorbell. Though that habit may not be the safest, especially in this day and age, as our neighborhood is relatively safe I did not give safety much thought. Each time I heard the doorbell ring, I just yelled, "Come in!"

This time Craig was at the door. Craig, his wife Sally Don, and their family have been our close friends and neighbors for many years; we also attend the same church. I heard Craig struggling to open the door, and as it swung open, I saw that his arms were full of casserole dishes covered with aluminum foil and plastic wrap.

"What on earth are you carrying? Do you need any help?" I asked.

"Don't get up; I got it," Craig answered. "Sally Don made a few things for you while Sherry was in Chicago. I'm just dropping them by. Here is some dinner for you tonight and an egg casserole for breakfast tomorrow," he continued.

"Craig, you didn't have to do this," I said as I watched him place the dishes on the kitchen counter.

"Are you kidding?" he replied. "After all that you and Sherry have done for us and our family over the years, now it's our turn to do something for you."

For one of the few moments in my entire life, I was speechless. But then I once more heard my parent's words, "Don't forget; someday you may need somebody to help you." Several times over the next two days until Sherry returned, friends and acquaintances of mine came one by one to see that I was okay and to help where needed.

My friends reminded me of an instruction that I once read in the Bible, "Do nothing from selfishness or conceit, but in humility count others greater than yourself" (Philippians 2:3). That exhortation is God's way of saying that, as he does not base his love for us on a balance sheet, neither should we use the balance sheet as a method of tallying what we do for others. Perhaps I found receiving so much more difficult for me than giving because, thanks to my parent's example, I have always considered the needs of others before myself with no strings attached. Therefore, when friends returned a favor without preconditions, the experience of God's unconditional love overwhelmed me with humility. As a result of the unconditional love all my dear friends showed me, I welled up with emotion when I was alone, then and even today. However, these emotional reflections do not spring from gratitude solely for the grace others showed me, but also for the wondrous example of compassion that my parents set for me. I truly miss them both.

Mobility Ridge

Only a few places existed that fifty feet of oxygen tubing would allow me to go. I did have the run of the first floor and most of the second floor of our house. I could also walk to the front porch and the rear deck and through the garage to my favorite chair just outside of the garage door where I liked to sit and drink my morning coffee. For the first two weeks that I was convalescing at home, the ability to experience even my oxygen-restricted world was such a joy mainly because the alternative, a hospital, was a place I wanted to forget!

The show in Chicago was a success, and much to my relief, the next day Sherry returned home. Although I was doing more each day to become as self-sufficient as possible, I still missed and needed her. My two days of self-sufficiency eventually led Sherry to decide to return to work and resume her normal schedule. I also wanted her to get back to a normal way of life so that she could stop worrying so much about me.

Staying home alone was not such a frightening prospect any more. My oxygen levels were getting so much better that I needed a shot of O^2 only when I was active. Even walking and climbing the stairs required fewer and fewer liters per minute of flow, about half what I needed the week before. All the improvement, however, caused another problem to develop. I developed a major case of cabin fever, and I needed to start spreading my wings just a bit.

I may have mentioned once or twice that I possess a great passion for cars. Since becoming empty-nesters, Sherry and I have enjoyed the blessing of being able to acquire a couple of collector cars that we like to drive and show. We have a 1976 convertible and a 1994 customized cruiser that we lowered as a retro example of an old street rod. We also joined a local and national collectors club, where we share our new hobby with other classic car enthusiasts.

If I had known what I know today when we built our house several years ago, I would have designed it with fewer rooms and more garage space. As a result, we only have a two-car garage, which would be fine for my two beauties if Sherry didn't need a garage space for her car. Consequently, I can only keep one of my toy cars at home while I store the other at a nearby self-storage unit. Because the self-storage unit is heated and air conditioned, in the winter I keep the older car in there and the newer one in our garage. I also drive an ugly old Volvo on my daily commute, but it does not need garaging and stays in the driveway.

I usually switch toy cars at the first sign of cruising weather in the spring, bringing the convertible home and putting the other in storage. However, because of my illness and hospitalization, I had left my toy cars in their winter configurations. Most people think that the convertible would be our favorite car, but we favor the newer one. It was the first car that we acquired as a specialty/collector car, and we call it the *Baby*.

As Sherry returned to her normal routine, I tried my best to create some semblance of a normal routine as well. Before my hospital experience, my daily routine during nice weather was to grab a cup of coffee and, with Katie leading the way, walk through the garage to my favorite chair just outside of the garage to enjoy the morning. However, the daily routine of the past two weeks of laps and stairs limited me to stopping by the door leading into the garage to glance admiringly at my *Baby.* These glances left me with a longing for the day when I could drive it again. Each day as I gradually re-acclimated to the old routine, just walking past my *Baby* evolved into opening its door, then to sitting in it, and then finally to starting it. The sound of the engine and the feel of the driver's seat made me want so badly to drive again, and to drive my *Baby*. I needed another plan!

I kept mum about what I was plotting to do later that week; I had to be silent. If I told Sherry that I was going to take the *Baby* out for a drive, she would hide the keys and chain me to the couch! So I began to hatch another secret plan to give me the confidence to move beyond the confines of my home.

Once again, first things first, I needed to ensure that I could breathe. The medical supply company had installed, in addition to the oxygen pump, a number of portable oxygen bottles of various sizes that I could use for short excursions away from home. One of these devices was a compact bottle in a carrying case, which resembled a school backpack. This device was very inconspicuous, inconspicuous enough that I could lay it on the floorboard by my feet where no one could see it. As I had progressed so much that I no longer required oxygen while sitting upright, I plotted to keep the O^2 tucked out of sight on the floorboard by my feet. In the event that I got lightheaded, I planned to reach down and take a few puffs of oxygen, and I would be all right. Besides, I do not think that the sight of a nasal cannula stuck in my nose would go over well if I was pulled over by a police officer!

Now that I had taken care of the oxygen issue, I needed to decide where I would drive. Even though you may think that what I planned to do was not one of my more brilliant ideas, I can assure you that I remained well aware of my limitations and the risks involved. I obviously did not plan a long drive in the country.

My local bank is about five or six blocks from home and away from any high-traffic areas. I needed to do some banking; so I decided that my first excursion away from home on my own would be to the drive-through facility of our bank to take care of a bit of business and then straight back home.

On the day of my reunion with the *Baby,* Sherry left for work a couple of hours before I began to hatch my plan. I walked into the garage with the aid of my portable oxygen bottle, opened the door of the car, and sat down. Before I pushed the button on the garage door opener, I removed the cannula and sat for a few moments to make sure that I was not dizzy. The final arbiter, however, of whether I would proceed or not was going to be the reading on my pulse-oximeter. *Ninety-four! Okay, open the garage door, start the engine, and pull to the end of the driveway. Read the pulse-ox again. Ninety-four! You're good to go!* At the first stop sign in our neighborhood, I took another reading on the pulse-ox; I was still at ninety-four and still good to go. Each time I came to a stop sign or stopping point, I glanced at the pulse-ox, which read ninety-four each time.

The entire trip there and back took no more than ten minutes, but for the first time in over a month, I felt a sense of liberation. Risky as my jaunt may have seemed, the confidence that I gained from this ten-minute excursion convinced me that I would not spend the rest of my life as an oxygen-sucking invalid. When I told Sherry later that night what I had done, instead of chastising me, she smiled and said without skipping a beat, "Good for you, hon; I guess this means you'll be able to go to church this Sunday."

So engrossed had I been in my adventure of the morning the thought had never crossed my mind that I could indeed return to church, and that next Sunday, I did. The summit of Mount Full Recovery was now in sight, but I still had one more obstacle to climb.

Dump the Pump Cliff

Nonetheless, my walking into church that following Sunday morning took a bit of doing. I still depended on some source of supplemental oxygen, which I got from the portable backpack-like bag and small bottle. I also needed a bit of extra time to get from place to place, as walking was still a slow and deliberate task for my post-atrophied legs to accomplish.

Consequently, Sherry and I entered the sanctuary a few minutes past the start of the service. We proceeded to sit in the back pews while trying not to draw any attention to ourselves; however, our Pastor was not going to let us.

Customarily, our Pastor would not stop the service or alter its order to recognize anyone or anything that was not included in the program or planned in advance. This morning, however, he felt the need to make an exception. I cannot recall his exact words, but they went something like this.

> "Congregation, I don't normally stray from the order of our worship services to recognize anyone, but I need to make an exception. We are blessed to have Paul Ulasien back with us this morning after being at death's doorstep only a few short weeks ago. Let us be thankful for God's grace and mercy in answering our prayers for his return to us!"

I know that our Pastor did not intend to draw attention to me or to embarrass me. Although I was unaware at the time, he sat by my bedside the morning that I spiraled down to the brink of death and witnessed the direness of my situation. He also prayed over me as I gasped for air and tried to get someone to recognize that I was dying. As he confessed to me several months later, that morning in the hospital was a frightening reminder of a similar experience several years prior. In that particular situation, a member of his congregation was also in ICU on a CPAP machine and at the brink of death. However, in that instance, the person died. That loss partially explains why he felt so grateful to see me and why he felt compelled to break with routine to mention my return to services.

Regardless of his intent to celebrate my return to church and not to embarrass me, I was still embarrassed. As everyone turned to acknowledge my presence, many of the smiles quickly turned to shock and disbelief. The last time that anyone from the church had seen me about seven weeks ago, as ill as I was, I was still a strapping, rotund, and tanned picture of vitality. Now I must have looked somewhat emaciated, frail, and pale to them. The shock of this sudden transformation in my appearance caught many by surprise.

What was even more embarrassing, however, was the fact that I still had that blasted bottle of oxygen in tow and nasal cannula strapped to my head. After all my attempts to conceal this unwanted appendage, people still glanced at it immediately as they came to greet Sherry and me after services and welcome us back. That ordeal convinced me; I needed to heal enough so that I no longer relied on supplemental oxygen. I needed another plan, but this time a plan with a different purpose.

The sanctuary at First Baptist Church of Lawrence is aesthetically pleasing to the eye. Several massive arched wooden beams join a center intersection approximately thirty feet above the front altar and baptismal to support the high, angled ceiling. Behind the baptismal stand an array of pipes for the church's organ and a tall contemporary wooden cross that matches the interior of the church in color and design.

That cross has always been a focal point. Many times throughout a typical service, I stare at that cross and think about all that it means to me. That cross was also a focal point as I lay in the hospital just a few weeks earlier. In addition to all the other stimuli to survive and get out of the hospital, I also visualized that cross in my mind. I wanted to see that cross again, but now something else compelled me. I also wanted to be re-baptized, not out of fear as in my childhood, but because of grace. My next plan would have as its purpose to walk, unaided by nurses, walkers, and oxygen, into the baptismal below that cross to rededicate my life to God.

I had progressed to the point that I only needed oxygen while moving about or sleeping. The need for oxygen while moving was a given, as my lungs were still healing from the effects of my surgery and illnesses. My need for oxygen while sleeping, however, was prompted by fear. The night after my surgery was when I began to have breathing difficulties, and now an innate fear preyed on me that I may have the same problem during the night while my lungs were getting stronger. So this dependency became more of a psychological need than a physical one.

I began the plan to wean myself completely from supplemental oxygen very simply. A few weeks prior, when I started walking laps through the house and then up the stairs, I had to turn the flow of oxygen from the pump from 2l (liters per minute) to 5l. As time progressed, I continually tried to do more on fewer liters per minute. This plan worked very well, and as the days passed, I found that I could do more with less, just not without. If, however, I was going to reach the top of the baptismal, I needed to be able to do completely without.

That evening after church, I walked my normal lap routine, but I decided to take a few steps without the nasal cannula in my nose. Standing stationary with my trusty pulse-ox on my index finger, I removed the cannula and read ninety-one on the pulse-ox. *Not bad,* I thought to myself; so I decided to take a few steps and then take another reading: still ninety-one. I walked into the kitchen and back into the living room and then took another reading. This time I read ninety, which was a somewhat borderline result, but I still felt capable of continuing. I kept walking back and forth until I started to feel a bit lightheaded: *Eighty-eight, time to sit.*

Just as I had started the process of walking laps to regain my strength, I now completed laps without the aid of my oxygen pump to strengthen my lungs. Each day I did a bit more and walked a bit longer unaided. After a couple of weeks, I was able to go on short walks again with Katie and climb 15 Stairs Peak all without the aid of supplemental oxygen. Still, however, I had trouble getting over the hump of not taking oxygen while I slept. Even after going all day without a single liter of supplemental oxygen, I was petrified to go to bed without it. I tried the experiment a couple of times, but panic set in if I took a pulse-ox reading of ninety or ninety-one. In a panic, I would plug myself back into the pump.

Thankfully, after a week of trying, I slept an entire night without the nasal cannula. By the sixth week of my home convalescence, my doctor gave his permission to the oxygen supply company to remove all the apparatuses from my home. The peaceful silence of not hearing that darned pump running twenty-four hours a day was a wonderful respite.

I was getting closer and closer to the summit of Mt. Full Recovery and Normalcy. Throughout the next ten weeks of summer, my physical capabilities began to return to normal. I still had a great deal of work to do, and I required many more weeks of physical therapy. But just like Mt. Standing on my Own Two Feet, Disappointment Ridge, Fifteen Stairs Peak, Humility Heights, Mobility Ridge, and Dump the Pump Cliff, Mt. Full Recovery and Normalcy was about to return to a mere molehill.

On that cool August Sunday morning as I stood on the top step of the baptismal looking down into the waters where the Pastor waited for me, I thanked God for the wonderful journey that I had just taken months prior and for his being with me every step of the way. That top step was the summit of Mt. Full Recovery and Normalcy, and the time had come to descend into the renewing waters of God's grace.

Chapter 12

Perspective

Close your eyes for a few moments and visualize standing in the most beautiful place you have ever imagined. Now turn in a virtual three-hundred-sixty-degree circle, all the while taking mental photographs of what you observe. Jot a few of these images on a piece of paper. Regardless of the fact that you may have never been to this place or may have seen it through a video or picture, you have still developed an image. That image is your perspective of the vista from that place. This perspective has an intrinsic significance. The point is not whether your perspective is accurate, but merely that you have one.

Perspective is a unique mental view or vista that you develop of an object or of a period of time. Your perspective of an object, perhaps like the summit of a tall mountain, contains unique specifics pertaining to your mental vista. Which of its aspects did you jot on your piece of paper? If you saw a mountain summit, you may have visually identified specifics such as snow, clouds, other peaks in the distance, etc.

Your mental view or vista of your past and present is the perspective of your life. Your perspective of a period of time depends on your existence as an individual. In your mental view or vista of the present and past are the many things that you can identify: people, places, things, and both good and bad times. This perspective is unique to you and you alone.

However, all of the specifics that you can identify within your perspective are only part of the whole of your identity. Identity is the foundation upon which we build perspective. The view or vista of your identity is paramount to the perspective image of your life.

The Nature of Identity

Popularized during the 1960s, the idea of having an identity developed as an effort to separate oneself from others. The goal of this separation was for the individual to decide personally what values to hold and what goals to pursue. However, noted psychologists of the era believed that the work of achieving an identity could come undone, particularly if a person were to become disillusioned or disassociated from his values and goals. People without a strong sense of identity are easy followers, experimenting with the ideals or causes of the moment while they allow an identity deficit to develop.

Deficits occur when a person who has no formulated identity struggles with the concept of what he is versus who he is. At the points of major decisions, a deficit will cause him to search abstract concepts or ideas for answers. The basic need to develop an identity has led many to fall victim to movements and cult thinking that promise much but deliver nothing other than more promises. For example, one such metaphysical program presents the idea that a person can understand and apply in his or her life the natural and universal ideals that govern the body, mind, and soul. This program promises that you will be at peace with yourself and the world and enjoy health instead of illness and abundance instead of poverty. Oh, by the way, any interested seeker can fulfill his needs for the mere price of subscribing to a thirty-five dollar annual membership, buying the program books and videos, and attending the seminar sessions.

Having a person or program developing your identity for a price can hardly lead to a foundation of strength and conviction, especially in regards to making life decisions. Falling prey to shallow ideals and abstract thinking based on a concept called suggestive therapy causes a lack of definition in values and goals. One cannot suggest his way into health, abundance, and peace. Suggestion is not reality. Reality admits that black is black and white is white. Trying to suggest to yourself otherwise will always keep reality beyond your reach and leave you a shallow and deficient life.

Making decisions, especially life decisions, requires the security of a foundation built on a conviction of inner and spiritual strength, not a suggestion. Going back to the definition of perspective (the mental view or vista of your past and present), your view or vista of your identity is paramount to your perspective. Consider making a life decision from a perspective built on a conviction of inner and spiritual strength to be like building a house on a foundation of granite. Making a life decision from a perspective of suggestive concepts would then be like setting the foundation of the house on silt and mud. A granite foundation will be reliable for ages, but silt and mud will wash away at the next suggestion.

The good news about identity is that it is not stamped on your forehead at birth. Identity develops over time and can change with time. Identity does not rely on others but on you. Earlier in this book, I described developing an identity from a balance-sheet mentality. My perspective dictated accepting the fact that good things in life were only the absence of me not screwing up. When bad things did happen, they signaled that God was getting back at me for something I probably could not remember doing wrong. My identity depended on the quid quo pro (this for that) philosophy. No matter what I did, right or wrong, I lived under the suggestive fear that if I upset the balance sheet I would suffer the consequences.

Fortunately I changed, and so did my identity. A stark reminder of my balance sheet perspective and identity appeared recently when I connected through a social networking website with an old college friend, Bob. Bob's last recollection of me was after our college days and during my second divorce. I was a basket case at the time, making decisions and doing stupid things based on experimenting with different identities as if these identities were hats, trying to see which one would fit. In his posting on my social network webpage, Bob asked, "How are you doing? I've worried about you over the years, because you were always so down and discouraged about your life." WHOA, talk about a chilling reminder of my old identity!

The shock that I experienced as a result of Bob's perception of me illustrates a feature of identity called **continuity.** Continuity means that people perceive you to be the same person today as you were the last time they interacted with you. Even though thirty years had passed, Bob's view or vista of me was the one of discouragement and discontent that he originally experienced.

As humans, we are susceptible to change, which is the antithesis of continuity. Though qualities such as gender, ethnicity, and your name remain stable over time, the identity, which is rooted in personality, will change. This second feature of identity is called **contrast.** Contrast means that your identity can change over time and differentiate your past from your present.

Side by side, the two features of identity obviously conflict. Continuity indicates the perception that we never change, but contrast indicates that we do. This paradox is why having an identity built on a solid foundation of conviction and strength versus suggestive concepts is so crucial. Identity continuity means that you are secure and confident in who you are. You base your decisions upon your convictions, and you have the strength to accept the outcomes. A contrasting identity means that you are insecure in your values and ideals. You make your decisions with difficulty, and you are full of apprehension once you have made them.

Developing a sense of continuity in your identity also gives continuity to your perspective. Confidence in who you are and in the decisions that you make allows you to have a perspective that your past is not fatal and your future is not final. The struggle to be the same person today and tomorrow as you were yesterday may seem improbable, but you can accomplish it. The place in which to find that continuity is the favor of God's grace. Grace is where you will find your continuity, and through grace you will minimize your contrasts.

The foundation upon which each is built provides the evidence that continuity comes from grace and not from abstract concepts and suggestive therapeutics. Based on the definition that continuity means never changing, grace is unequivocally the answer. Dr. Patrick Morley once described the modern view of God as, "There is the God we want, and there is the God who is, and they are not the same God."[3] God is the same, yesterday, today, and for all eternity.

Despite man's tireless efforts to make God something other than he really is, only he represents a universal continuity.

Abstract and suggestive therapeutic programs such as Dianetics, Concept-Therapy, and Gestaltism cannot make the same claim to continuity. Programs such as these have foundations based on evolving ideals and practices. They are not the same today as they were yesterday, and they will morph into something different in future. These programs epitomize contrasting insecurities full of apprehension.

If you are so inclined and have access to the Internet, a visit to the websites of some of the aforementioned suggestive therapeutic programs to experience firsthand a complete absence of continuity would be worth your time. These programs are designed to immerse you so far in their concepts that you will make a hundred leaps of identity trying to find the one hat that fits.

Grace, on the other hand, requires you to base your identity on only two truths. The first is an understanding of who you are. You are the child of God, a God who never changes. The names of God in the ancient Greek and Hebrew language support this assertion. The Greeks referred to God as *Theos,* meaning one true or singular God. Among their many names for God, the Hebrews referred to God as *Elohim,* meaning strong one or strength. The Hebrew name of God that truly embodies his continuity over time is *Jehovah,* which we translate to mean "I Am that I Am." He has never been something different than what he is now, nor will he be something different as time passes. He is the same yesterday, today, and forever. Now that is continuity.

The second truth about grace on which you can base your identity is that the God who never changes one iota passionately loves you! When I was a child, I had no concept of the depth or breadth of love that a parent can have for a child. Only after my sons were born did I come to realize this type of love. If you are a parent, you will know what I mean, and if you are not yet a parent, perhaps one day you will be. Parental love is an amazing yet overwhelming emotion that we cannot put into words but only experience. Take that passion and multiply by one million, and you still could not come close to how much God loves each of us.

I could not sacrifice either of my sons to die on a cross just to pardon a bunch of lowly and whiny sinners! I am too selfish and weak in spirit to allow that fate for my boys. Only God has the capacity of love to allow his Son to die in his presence for someone else's benefit. He also brooks no contrast in loving one person more than another. He loves us all the same as if we were his one and only child.

You are a child of God, who passionately loves you. You have no need for a webpage full of meaningless books, videos, and seminars which suggest that you are something other than the person God sees. Building your identity on the simple principles of grace is not a difficult proposition, because sometimes less can be more.

The Four Myths of Identity

The foundation upon which you build your identity is paramount to the perspective of your values, goals, and decisions. If you are irrefutably confident in who you are, then regrets from past decisions and actions will not matter, because you have the strength to accept those outcomes and the wisdom to learn from your mistakes and move forward. On the other hand, if you harbor persistent doubts about your past, these doubts will fester and harm your future. Many people in such a predicament will actually decide to abandon their goals as they experience an identity deficit from a lack of continuity. None of the hats from programs or ideals of suggested identities have ever fit. The stark reality that one size does not fit all comes into view as promises from a program continually deliver disappointment.

In the scheme of identity, believing that health, abundance, and peace are merely a few clicks of a mouse or a few turns of a page away is as substantive as a screen door on a submarine (pardon the colloquial analogy). Seriously, the mythical promises of suggestive therapies and ideals are incompatible with the universal need for continuity of identity. Here are four general concepts among the many metaphysical programs that are myths with respect to the formulation of identity and ultimately perspective.

Myth one - image is everything. Oh, really? How you look, act, dress, and conduct yourself defines you as a person? The ageless adage that beauty is only skin deep should suffice as an adequate analogy to debunk the suggested importance of image. Regrettably, our pop-culture-oriented society continuously bombards us with the shallow ideal of image. The media, entertainment, and marketing industries thrive on skewing reality when they present an image of how people should look and behave.

Imagine if you will a species of beings from another galaxy that have intercepted TV broadcasts from earth and decided to seek this glamorous species of millionaires with trim waistlines, clear complexions, and full heads of hair. Think of their shock and disappointment when they encounter a bunch of pot-bellied, pock-marked, thin-haired, middle-class Joes and Janes. They would probably think they took a wrong turn at the last black hole. In perfect candor, as benign and nonsensical as this analogy may seem, it does illustrate this myth in perspective. The view or vista that this alien culture encountered in reality was not what they were led to believe. If you have an identity that presents your image as something other than your true character, others will think that they took wrong turn somewhere when the real person emerges from that false image.

A great deal of what the media and institutions try to suggest is that self-esteem relates in direct proportion to self-image. They suggest that an image of success, prosperity, and beauty will produce a feeling of high self-esteem. The subliminal message that lies beneath the suggestion of glitz and glamour is that image must be had for a price. You can seriously damage your self-esteem if you do not become the image you just purchased for $19.95. Anxiety and fear of failure may cause the opposite of the suggested image, actually producing a low self-esteem. As the late Dr. Martin Luther King once said, we should be "judged not by the color of our skin but by the content of our character."[4] The same can hold true for your identity and perspective. Beauty is only skin deep, and what truly identifies you is not the image that lies on the surface but the character that shines beneath it.

Myth two – what truly matters is not what you believe but what you do. Okay, living by the golden rule of doing unto others as you would have them to unto you is a noble and worthy goal. We should all strive to fulfill this ideal. The problem arises from the motivation with which a person performs good works.

Recently, I participated in a rigorous discussion with an acquaintance as to the merits of people who perform good deeds. My acquaintance was convinced that the key to going to heaven was not having a personal relationship with God but being a good person and doing good things for others.

"Okay," I said, "that's all well and good, but what is the baseline of what constitutes a good deed?"

"Well," my friend replied, "there is only one kind of good; so I am not sure what you mean."

I gave the following example to explain my point. Consider a person who is the head of a local bank. The economic conditions at the time are not good, and this person is in a quandary. Does he decide to keep the bank solvent until the economic tides turn, or does he seize an opportunity to make a windfall profit now? Hanging in the balance of this decision is the fate of a hundred mortgages in delinquency or the price per share of a hundred shareholders. If the banker decides to work with the customers who are struggling to make their mortgage payments, the bank can still keep its doors open but barely break even. However, if he forecloses on the delinquent mortgages and sells the seized assets to an investor, he can turn the deal of the century to increase the price per share of the bank's stock a thousand percent.

Regardless of the decision the banker makes, a hundred people will consider it brilliant, while the other hundred people will consider the decision foolhardy or heartless. My friend looked at me with a blank stare and had no response.

Doing something that on the surface may appear to be a good deed to one person could have the opposite appearance to another. Decisions based on the complexity of a situation are decisions of rationale. Weighing the rationale of good and bad outcomes to an action only produces a result and does not quantify a baseline for a good deed. Sir Isaac Newton's third law of motion states that for every action there is an equal and opposite reaction. No baseline in this law of motion constitutes whether the reaction is positive or negative; it states only that a reaction occurs. Equally, the rationale of weighing the good or bad reactions of a deed also lacks a baseline.

The baseline for determining a good deed is the motivation behind the act itself. People daily perform thousands of deeds with good intentions, but they also daily perform thousands of deeds that are of circumstantial intent. Some choose to act because doing so is right and just, versus doing something because they can.

The quandary of the motivation behind a deed lies in the source from whence it emanates. C.S. Lewis very succinctly addressed this quandary in his description of the three components of morality.[5] First is the concept of fair play and harmony between individuals. This concept echoes the golden rule, treating people as you would like to be treated. This concept is not difficult to grasp, and it can be universally applied.

The second concept, tidying or harmonizing your soul, is where we begin to lose a few individuals. Fair play and harmony between individuals is an action predicated on a sense of feeling good about a situation. However, such actions rely on an individual's need for conveyance without conviction. People will perform a deed to avoid causing disharmony or conflict because their identity lacks continuity. Contrasts will infiltrate their decisions, and they will react only in the moment with no regard to consistency.

The third and final of C.S. Lewis' components of morality is the general purpose of human life and why we exist. In my first job out of college, I worked as a technical draftsman for a consulting engineering company that designed power plants. The drawings that were part of my work had many intricate components, such as the nuts and bolts that held the steel superstructure of the plant together. Each nut and bolt had to be individually numbered and identified, yet in the purpose of the greater design of the power plant these components existed as a collective contribution to the plant's creation of electrical energy.

In the realm of infamous engineering disasters, many times a failure in the most insignificant part of a whole can set into motion a chain of events that can lead to a catastrophe. Our morals and values are no different. As our cultures have begun the process of ceding morality for the sake legality, the fabric of human life and our existence has started to unravel. As C.S. Lewis most aptly wrote, "You cannot make good men by law, and without good men you cannot have a good society."[6]

When we stop at the concept of fair play and harmony to establish a baseline for what constitutes a good deed, we grease the slippery slope of our declining culture. Here are a few examples. Declaring school prayer unconstitutional may placate those who loudly advocate the contrived notion of the separation of church and state, but since that ruling, what has happened to the state of public education? Enabling the no-fault divorce laws may have simplified the messiness, embarrassment, and complexity of a contested divorce, but what has happened to the state of marriage and the family since then? Legalizing abortions may support one interpretation of the constitutional rights to life, liberty, and the pursuit of happiness, but what has happened to the concepts of personal responsibility and the value of human life since then? The answers to these questions refer to what C.S. Lewis said, "You cannot make good men by law, and without good men you cannot have a good society."

And the fact that something has been legalized in many instances still does not make it right. First the cohesiveness of humanity begins to decay, and we begin to overreact with our heads and ignore the callings of the heart. Once that process of desensitization has been set into motion, the guidance of our deeds becomes a matter of procedure rather than character, inner reliance on the soul and spirit.

Myth three - likability is better than sensibility. Everyone wants to be well-liked and respected; these desires are natural components of human emotion. What is unnatural is the extent to which some will go to be well-liked and respected.

Each of us can relate to the emotions that likability and respect produce. Take a few moments to remember your days in high school. If your high school was anything like mine, everyone belonged to one of three distinct castes: popular, unpopular, or somewhere in between. The popular kids were Homecoming King and Queen and members of the student council, those cheerleaders, babes, and jocks who drove cool cars. The unpopular kids, largely ignored by the popular kids during school and social events, maintained their own social networks, such as chess and science club. I was one of the in-betweeners. I had friends who were popular and friends who were anything but popular, and I vacillated between the two extremes. In the presence of the popular kids, I kept my unpopular friends at arm's length, but I hovered in the airspace of my unpopular friends when no one of importance was watching.

As hypocritical as being an in-betweener may have seemed, my emotional need for acceptance into the higher strata of the school's social hierarchy dented my sensibility. During the formative years of a child's life, the consuming need of acceptance can override the hurt that it may cause others. For most of us, the need for acceptance dims somewhat as we mature emotionally and develop a sense of confidence and self-reliance. However, for others the need for acceptance becomes so ingrained into their psyche that they will go to any and all extremes to fill their insatiable void of self-confidence.

An identity formulated on the idea that being liked is better than being sensible surrenders to contrast rather than standing on continuity. People who are obsessed with being liked refuse to allow the formative emotion of need to wane naturally with maturity. An idea of who they are trying to be supplants who they really are. Dressing to impress, driving flashy cars, buying opulent homes, chasing professional titles, and flaunting social status can demonstrate a burning need for acceptance.

Although many people have nice clothes, cars, homes, jobs, and respect, they obtain these things over time with a modicum of patience and planning. The obsession with possessions and titles divides people who want to be the center of constant attention from people who are confident in who they are. Some psychological issues can explain this obsession for attention, such as narcissistic and histrionic personality disorders, but in other cases, just as I was in my high school days as an in betweener, attention seeking can result from hypocrisy, which is not our purpose in life.

In the New Testament book of Matthew, Jesus speaks to his apostles about the issue of drawing attention to one's self as an act of hypocrisy. Giving to the needy out of humility and compassion is preferable to fanfare and public proclamations of philanthropy. God disdains those who trumpet their charity to draw attention to themselves rather than give out of the goodness of their hearts. Hypocrites cannot bamboozle God by acts done merely to stroke the ego. God knows what is in your heart even before you do.

Likability does need to correlate with acceptance, not the acceptance of an identity that is based on what you are trying to be, but acceptance based on security in who you really are. If you are secure in your identity, then you will view quality dress, nice cars, beautiful homes, professional titles, and social status as gifts from God rather than possessions or obsessions. People will accept you for who you are. Moreover, if they cannot handle your real identity, do not worry, because God can.

Myth four –don't worry; be happy. I have to admit that what inspired my formulation of myth four is the title of the Bobby McFerrin's 1980s hit song, "Don't Worry; Be Happy."[7] The words in this song encourage a person to look beyond the daily travails of life to the bright side beyond and be happy. As one of the lyrics states, "In your life / expect some trouble /but when you worry / you make it double / don't worry / be happy." This lyric does have some truth. We can all attest to the fact that life is not a smooth road to travel and that a preoccupation with worrying can amplify the problem. However, you cannot just happy a problem away by ignoring its reality.

In the world of politics, the old adage of "kicking the can down the road" aptly describes what I am trying to illustrate with the phrase: "don't worry; be happy." Politicians love to defer problems to another day until another generation has to solve them. Most entitlement programs begin with good intentions but, unfortunately, without any semblance of sustainability. Buy now and pay later political philosophies are pushing many countries, including ours, towards the brink of bankruptcy as we draw closer to the end of the road and inevitability run out of room to kick the can.

A "don't worry; be happy" identity may create the impression of a person who is open, conscientious, and agreeable. Hidden behind this veiled view, however, are shallowness, denial, and possibly neuroses. Wishing for happiness at the expense of ignoring inevitability does not work. Happiness requires hard work to achieve. To be happy, a person must work to overcome the problems, losses, and failures that constitute reality. The "don't worry; be happy" attitude buys happiness now and pays dearly for it later. In order to succeed, you have to pay as you go.

Erik Erikson was a twentieth century developmental psychologist and psychoanalyst known for his theory on social development of human beings, and he became most famous for coining the term "identity crises."[8] During his career, Erikson's main body of work involved his theory of the eight stages of psychosocial development through which a healthily developing human should pass from infancy to late adulthood. The first seven stages of development, also called the life-stage virtues, occur in the following periods of development:

1) Hope – infancy

2) Will – toddler
3) Purpose – kindergarten
4) Competence – age six to puberty
5) Fidelity – teenager
6) Love – young adult
7) Caring – the mid-life crises

The previous seven stages culminate in the eighth and final stage of development which occurs in old age: Wisdom. During this final stage, a perspective of integrity versus despair develops as an individual defines his or her journey through the previous seven stages. Faced with the specter of more days behind than ahead, a person in the final stages of life takes stock of his or her accomplishments and failures, thereby setting the stage for how he or she will live the remainder of their life. Individuals with a perspective of integrity will find comfort in their memories and will view their lives with satisfaction. They will actually handle the prospect of death quite well without the burden of regret. However, despair in this final stage will cause bitterness and dissatisfaction with unreached goals, which engender preoccupation with death and obsessive fear of it.

A "don't worry; be happy" attitude or a buy now and pay later mentality through the earlier stages of development causes the identity crises that Erikson described in his work. Like maxing out a credit card, eventually the bill comes due, and it must be paid. The book of Proverbs says that a person who puts little to no effort into life's journey or does not plow in season looks at harvest time or the end of life and finds nothing but despair (Proverbs 20:4). Sadly, this scenario leaves no room for happiness.

Overcoming in the face of adversity or paying as you go through life may not maintain a state of constant happiness, but grace both lightens your burdens and makes you strong enough to bear them. One of my favorite sayings is "When things get tough, God will not get you around trouble; he will get you through it." Earlier in this book, I wrote of my mother's reference to the part of life she called heartache and sorrow. As difficult as I can imagine that heartache and sorrow was for her to bear, I witnessed how God's grace got her through it and how grace can work for everyone.

I am not trying to depress you with the prospect that each of us will have to deal with adversity in our lives. Adversity is a part of life that we cannot avoid by just being happy. Ignoring reality will only lead to an identity crisis from which we may not recover. However, when you relinquish to God's grace your desire to control your life, he may just surprise you with a pot of unanticipated happiness at the end. God never promised that life would be easy, but without grace your identity and ultimately your perspective may leave you nothing but despair.

Be happy in who you are, comfortable in what you believe, sensible in how others view you, and face life's challenges as they come. Being faithful in your image, beliefs, likability, and happiness defines your character, identity, and perspective. Consistency will never be easy, but in the end it will definitely be worth the effort.

Chapter 13

The Power of a Grace Perspective

Each time that I tell the story of my brush with death, listeners always respond immediately in the same way: “Oh my God, that must have been terrible,” or “You’ll probably want to forget about that, now that it’s behind you.” Can you imagine their reaction when I respond by saying, “Actually, it was the most wonderful experience of my life, and if I could return to change any part of it, I would change none of it!” After that answer, I can guarantee that most people are probably thinking: *This guy must be an order of fries short of a value pack meal*, but that is to be expected. I can very easily describe the events of what happened to me in April and May of 2005; however, equally difficult to describe are the experiences. To that end, when I tell my story, I only focus on what is easy to describe and do not wax philosophical. I reserve that luxury for the context of this book!

So what was so wonderful about my experiences that I would not change a single part of it? The explanation refers to the Ursula K. Le Guin quote that I mentioned at the end of chapter three,

> *"It is good to have an end to journey toward,*
> *But it is the journey that matters in the end."*

Whenever I read this quote, I sense that what Ms. Le Guin may have meant when she said *"but it is the journey that matters in the end"* is that not only our journey but our **perspective** of the journey matters as well.

Consider my perspective of the events and experiences that I have described in this book if I had an identity that accentuated only the negative aspects of the events rather than the positive experiences during my illness, surgery, and recovery. I might more aptly have titled this book something like "The Pitfalls of Unhealthy Habits and the Shortcomings of the American Healthcare System." The **power of a grace perspective** allows us to view events and experiences with the ability to forget what lies behind and reach forward to what lies ahead. The age-old adages of seeing a glass half empty or half full, being unable to see the forest for the trees, or looking for the silver lining in a dark cloud all apply to the same concept of the **power of a grace perspective.**

God gives us the free will to make our own decisions. Invoking free will in the decision-making process also leaves us in control of the perspective gained from the events and experiences that result from our free-will decisions. Finally, the aspects of the results on which we chose to focus determine whether our perspective will indeed be a glass half empty or a glass half full.

I could very easily have taken a woe-is-me perspective from my experiences in the hospital and during convalescence. That view, however, would have been an affront to God after all that he did for me. How could I diminish to a mere happenstance of events the string of miracles, his presence when I awoke, his assurance that I was not alone, the dreams he sent, and the courage that he gave me to overcome all the molehills that became mountains?

What I did, not what God dictated, resulted in the dire circumstances that led to my hospitalization and nearly dying three times. My bad decisions over a lifetime put me into the situation from which God's grace delivered me. However, I am still in charge of the perspective that I took from this experience. I could say either, "Woe is me," or "I am blessed." I picked the latter.

Have I ever had a woe-is-me perspective? Absolutely - at one period in my life when I was transitioning from my balance sheet upbringing and I still carried the baggage of a glass-half-empty perspective, cynicism and arrogance ruled my attitudes. The churches that I was forced to attend made me very cynical about the empirical importance of God. To me, if God and the church were so narrow minded that only seven hundred out of six and a half billion souls would go to heaven in the rapture, I could find little to no solace in believing that God cared about the remaining 6,499,999,300 of us. This cynicism led to the arrogant conclusion that I did not need God and that I could fend for myself. After all, in spite of how little he cared about me, at least he did give me a brain that I could use, and I would rely more on my abilities than God's grace.

Thankfully, my cynicism and arrogance did not hinder God's unconditional love and the availability of his grace when I was ready to receive it. As I matured (at least I hope that I have), my cynicism about God and my arrogance towards him began to wane. Brief snippets of grace would permeate random thoughts, and I started to see a side of God that had no balance sheet attached.

Until his death, my father continued to badger me about going to the Branham-centric church that he insisted was the one true church. I instead consciously chose to seek those who saw God as I was beginning to see him and worship with them. I desired only the unconditional love that is with me even to the end of the age!

Periods versus Question Marks

"Don't put a question mark in place of where God has put a period!" For the life of me, I cannot remember when or where I heard that quote, but I must have thought that it had some major significance, because I recorded it in my notes for this book. Well, voila, here it is, and how apropos! A most difficult task for some but an easy one for others is to put what is behind us that we cannot change into its proper perspective and move on. Alcoholics Anonymous most aptly reflects this task in their prayer:

God, grant me the serenity
To accept the things I cannot change;
Courage to change the things I can;
And wisdom to know the difference.[9]

Couple this prayer with the verse I had earlier paraphrased from the Bible, "Forgetting what lies behind and reaching forward to what lies ahead," and I think you should get the message of what God desires for us. My dreams provided evidence of that desire as well. Yet why do so many insist on sticking that proverbial question mark where a period belongs? The answer lies in Christ's lament: "O ye of little faith!" (Matthew 6:30).

Modern culture has become the fertile breeding ground for a cynicism and arrogance which have become so acute that even those considered most strong in their faith are allowing the poison to cloud their perspectives. Just look at the state of modern Christianity. Many churches are skewing further from redemption and more towards revenue. The holiest of Christian observances, Christ's birth and resurrection, no longer provide times of reflection and worship but merely opportunity for profit. Such lost sheep focus more on cash flow and revenue than evangelism and salvation. Many so-called mega-churches and televangelists are sucking the life blood out of country churches with extravagant productions meant to entertain rather than redeem. The end result is a vicious cycle of coveting higher cash flows with which to mount ever bigger productions to gain even more cash flow.

Christ said that "wherever two or three are gathered together in my name, I am in their midst" (Matthew 18:20), and God commands us to "be still and know that I am God" (Psalm 46:10). I hold nothing against mega-churches and televangelists per se; mind you, many large congregations and television ministries do not fall into that classification. However, we must consider whether we are using the church, mega, televised, or country, for its proper intent. I can best answer this question by paraphrasing a quote by Pastor Tim Keller, "God meant the church to be a hospital for sinners, not a museum for saints."[10]

We have all seen the obligatory annual surveys and poll results that purportedly gauge the spiritual mood of the country with the same old tired questions. "Do you believe in God?" (By the way, Satan believes in God; so what value does that question have?) "Do you attend church regularly, occasionally, or not at all?" The questions vary little and extend ad nauseam. Those polls are easy to conduct and to answer. In the next poll a research organization conducts to gauge the spiritual climate of the population, I would like to see some different questions. Instead of "Do you believe in God," why not ask, "Do you love God?" Or how about, "What comes first in your life, God, career, money, or another priority?" Talk about gauging the spiritual mood of the country! Unfortunately, therein lays the conundrum of faith versus arrogance and cynicism and how this paradox affects the power of a grace perspective.

The wonders of technology, science, and social evolution have caused us to focus more on outcomes than inputs **(faith)**. We are so indoctrinated to expect quick results **(arrogance)** that we ignore the stark reality that nothing in life comes easy. However, when stark reality finally does bop us upside the head, deep disappointment and doubt will follow **(cynicism).** Faith is the period; arrogance and cynicism are the question marks. Putting your faith in God, not the antithesis of God, allows you to put that period where it should be and move forward. Conversely, inserting the question marks will keep you mired in a lifetime of waning hope, devoid of answers.

The story of Job in the Old Testament and Hebrew Scriptures provides an excellent example of the dichotomy between periods and question marks and how it relates to faith versus arrogance and cynicism. Allow me to provide those of you who are not familiar with this story with a condensed version in a modern narrative.

The Perspective of Job

Job was a man of great wealth, stature, and power. Job was also a man of great faith and virtue. One day God and his adversary must have been sitting down for coffee discussing the universal grand scheme of things when the topic of Job arose. Apparently, the example that Job was setting was a burr in the adversary's saddle. The adversary told God, "Well, no wonder Job thinks that you are so great; he has everything that a person could ever want. I bet if life were not so peachy for your boy Job, it would be a different story!"

God responded, "You are wrong about Job, but knowing you, for the sake of argument you are going to want me to prove so."

"You bet," said the adversary.

God replied, "Okay, to prove my point that Job is a righteous and faithful man in spite of his good fortune, I will allow you to have your way with Job, with one exception: you cannot touch him physically."

Gleefully the adversary said, "You're on."

A series of calamities then came down on Job. Over a short period, Job's riches, his livestock, his house, and his servants were gone. In addition, Job also learned in a series of four messages that all his children had perished in various disasters. Reduced to rags, Job fell to his knees and prayed to God, "You gave me all that I have, and you have the right to take it all back. I am still blessed for all that I am!"

As you may be able to guess, the adversary did not care for that reaction. So he came back to God and said, "Well, okay, I'll give you that one, but Job is only suffering emotionally. I bet if he was hurting physically, it would be another story."

Confident in Job's strong sense of faith, God rescinded his previous conditions and allowed the adversary to touch Job physically, but only to the point of not killing him. Once again gleeful, the adversary agreed and quickly afflicted Job with many excruciatingly painful diseases. Having reduced Job to the lowest possible state of existence, the adversary also decided to add a couple of question marks to stack the deck in his favor. Besides all the maladies that Job suffered, now Job's wife began to chastise him and demand that he tell God to take a hike. Three of Job's closest friends also jumped onto the blame game wagon and told Job that his situation resulted from something evil that Job himself had done. God was merely punishing him for some past transgression. (Sound familiar? Remember the balance sheet?)

An argument ensued between Job and all the people tossing him question marks. Job refused to believe that God was out to get him, but you cannot help thinking that his faith was beginning to waver a bit as the question mark arguments permeated Job's thoughts. Job began to formulate a bit of a question mark by thinking to himself: *So God, why is this happening to me?*

Then God apparently had seen enough and decided to intervene. "Job, when you obtain the ability to create the moon, the sun, and the stars, then you will have the right to ask me why. In the meantime, what you need to do is to have faith in me and trust that what I am doing is best for you, all my creatures, and the world. Never again put a question mark where I have put a period!"

Job asked God to forgive him, and God restored his question marks to a new life ten times better than his previous one. The adversary silently slipped away in defeat.

Period people and question mark people are as distinct as day and night, and you do not have to go to church to find them. Just look around your workplace or circle of friends, and you will see them. I travel extensively during the course of a year, lecturing and teaching. In my travels, I also meet many people. Within a matter of minutes I can distinguish between period people and question mark people I have never before met. The congenial ones and the grouches: those labels describe them very well. One wants to be there, and one has to be there. The ones that want to be there are excited about the possibilities and opportunities. The ones that have to drag themselves there are just trying to square some artificially imposed balance sheet. The good news for all the question marks out there is that grace can take away the squiggle above the period in a question mark and help you to leave just the period.

As I experienced in my first waking moment from ten days on life support, God's presence is right there, flowing around you just a whisper away. Making that leap of faith to put arrogance and cynicism behind is life altering, believe me. We and we alone can decide to place God first and to put all other things in their proper places.

Manipulators of a Grace Perspective

A church or a leader of faith should only act as a guide to strengthening a relationship with God, but never a proxy. On one of my recent lecture trips to Springfield, Missouri, I returned to my hotel room after 10:00 pm and decided to relax by channel surfing for something interesting to watch on TV. As anyone who has ever been to Springfield knows, this city is the headquarters for several fundamental Christian denominations, and it probably has more religious programming on TV than any other city you may ever visit.

Going from channel to channel, I saw a couple sitting in a configuration like a Regis and Kelly talk show with an audience surrounding them. I stopped on this channel because something seemed vaguely familiar about one of these people, and I became perplexed as to what bothered me. Suddenly I began to recall images from the 1980s of a TV evangelist and his ding-a-ling wife/sidekick in a similar setting. This recollection of the 1980s also brought forth images of the financial empire built by this so-called faith leader through his pitch for people to give him money to build a theme park in the name of God. Fortunately for us, his dalliances with a staff worker in his empire led to his fall from grace to disgrace and eventually into jail.

"OH-MY-GOD," I yelled at the TV. The guy was the same guy but this time with a new ding-a-ling sidekick. And guess what? Instead of pitching theme parks to his vanity, he was now hawking real estate to the same end: a planned combination faith community and lake resort!

I broke aloud into laughter as I saw this pitiful man still hung up on his ego and trying to build a monument to himself. Then pure shock silenced my laughter. There in the audience surrounding this sideshow act appeared the faces of men and women intrigued by the guile of his message. They also had an eerie look of willingness to plunk down their hard-earned savings to stroke this guy's insatiable ego.

My shock soon turned to rage as I began to listen to his pitch and how he began to twist the Bible to serve his vanity. I had to temper my anger briefly as I scrambled frantically about the room for a pad and pencil so that I could write down what he said. Here it is paraphrased:

> *"God said in the book of Revelation that the end of the age is a time of harvesting [i.e. your money] for the church and its people. These are the fruitful days for us, and we need to be in obedience to God's promise of harvesting for the church before the great tribulation."*

Can you believe it? And even worse, can you believe that people are gullible enough to fall for this kind of crapola again and again and again? "O ye of little faith!"

God is good, and God is simple. Theme parks, faith-based lake resorts, and multi-million dollar crystal cathedrals of vanity are not where you go to find God. He is sitting with you right at this moment as your read this book. He is there with you as you laugh and as you cry. God is with you now and always, even to the end of the age. So stop looking for him where he is not, so that you can replace your question mark with a period and move on. Your perspective on your life and the goodness of God's grace depend on accepting his presence.

Chapter 14

Applying the Power of a Grace Perspective

One nice thing about perspective, unlike what lies behind us, is that perspective is not etched into stone. Perspective can evolve and change over a lifetime or even overnight. Before my hospital stay, my perspective had been evolving for the better, from balance sheet influences to unconditional love and grace. However, some times in our lives can deliver our perspectives a jolt, intended or unintended. I received such a jolt when I woke from ten days at the brink of death. Some profound changes in my life and perspective have occurred since that day.

Now or Maybe Never

Life is short. Though I know how clichéd that statement must sound, it so true, and it sounds so profound if you have spent a bit of time at the brink of death. Life does eventually come to an end. For some the end comes sooner than later, but regardless of timing, the end does come. While we are engrossed in the middle of life, we tend to ignore its finality. After all, always worrying about death would not be healthy for anyone's psyche. That fear would just get in the way of living. However, a certain beneficial perspective can accrue from almost dying, and I would like to share it with you.

Before teetering at the brink of death, I have to admit that I was somewhat of a procrastinator. I commonly put off chores like yard work or projects such as writing or business initiatives. Remember, I was that low stress easy going kind of a guy who rolled with the punches. Not anymore. I may not have tomorrow, and all that I want to do may never happen unless I get started. I now have a purpose in all that I do and, unlike before, a pure joy in doing it.

So now, how do I deal with the stress? I have learned that I created many of the stresses that I felt in past situations through a lack of diligence and faith in God's willingness to help me through those situations. When I came to grips with the finality of life and the importance of time being of the essence and the essence of time, I began to **do** rather than **put off.** I no longer have the worry of undone things hanging over my head! I could have avoided all those years of dealing with stress through artificiality merely by dealing expeditiously with it through God rather than just anesthetizing it. How simple was that?

Getting things done before I assume room temperature for the final time is not the only perspective that I gained from realizing that life is short. My relationships with family, friends, and strangers have changed as well. Those who know me also know that I am a friendly and open person to people who I know and to people whom I have just met for the first time. I have always been quick to wave as I pass or as people pass me. Coming face to face with the realization of how short life is, however, has changed that reflex somewhat. I do less waving these days and a great deal more stopping. By this I mean that, instead of driving through the neighborhood, seeing an old friend or neighbor, waving to him, and moving on, I now take the time to stop and talk.

Who knows? I may never have the opportunity to talk with that person again, and you would be amazed at the therapeutic value that stopping and talking has over just waving. Smiles begin to appear on people's faces, and even for a brief period of the day, the hustle and bustle of life takes a break. You get the opportunity to reconnect with someone with whom you may have had a waning friendship. You may even get a cup of coffee out of the deal or maybe a nice cool drink to enjoy. You would be surprised at how little time it takes away from your day and how much it adds to you as a person just to stop for a few minutes versus waving as you pass.

Blessings Are in the Eye of the Beholder

Our days on earth may be numbered, but the blessings that we receive each day are not. In every moment of the day from waking until falling back to sleep, I find an abundance of blessings that I once ignored or took for granted. My first act every morning is to thank God for letting me wake to enjoy another day. My second is usually to thank him that I can walk from the bed without a walker, wheelchair, or oxygen tube. This habit may sound a bit kooky to you, but I can assure you that it is God's honest truth. Realistically, I do not spend my entire day thanking God for every breath and every step that I take. That would be kooky! Nonetheless, I certainly am more aware of all the little things that I once thought to be minutia, and I recognize that they truly are blessings not only to prompt gratitude but also to enjoy.

I have always marveled at the beauty of sunrises, sunsets, clouds, and such, but since my brush with death, my senses have begun to absorb so much more of what I used to dismiss as just life and environment. Many things may seem insignificant to some of you, like a field of corn or the sun peeking through a cloud, but to me they have the same great significance as God's most spectacular vistas.

My new perception is very similar to the way a blind or deaf person's other senses become more acute to compensate for the loss of sight or hearing. Everything appears sharper to me in a similar way, only I also have the luxury of enjoying all my senses intact. Things that I never noticed before are now very distinct in all respects: sight, sound, smell, touch, and taste.

Just now, as I look to my left at the scene from my office window, the homes, trees, and foliage that have been there for more than twelve years look different every day. Each day, I see things outside my window that I had never seen before. These new sights and sounds have always been there, I am just more aware of them now. This awareness has also caused me to be more appreciative as well. Several times a day I find myself saying: *Thanks, God, for this,* or *Thanks, God, for that*. Before my illness, I doubt if I thanked God for much of anything during the course of a day. I was always too preoccupied with life to notice all the beauty and blessings that surrounded me. Just as God's presence surrounds us, so also does his creation, which can affect our perspective as well.

Looking at everything around and inside of us as a blessing rather than just happenstance does powerfully impact your perspective. In times of joy it will humble, and in times of grief it can comfort. This view was no truer for our family than just recently. Our precious lab-mix Katie girl went to be with the angels just a few short weeks before I wrote this passage, at the age of fifteen years and four months. But our family feels so blessed to have been able to experience those fifteen years and four months of joy and happiness. We miss our Katie girl with all our hearts, and a permanent emptiness has replaced her warm companionship. Nevertheless, through all the tears we have also smiled and laughed as we reminisced about how much joy she brought to our entire family and what a blessing in our lives this little angel was for so many years. Although I grieve at her loss, my perspective is so full of joy and happiness. Her love for us was unconditional, and therefore I know that she is in a place where unconditional love abounds. When my journey is finally complete, just like when I returned home from the hospital, my Katie girl will be there to greet me, and we will once more and forever take those long walks and chase rabbits like we only parted yesterday.

Dear God, thank you for your blessings, even for the ones that you have to take back. They still leave beautiful memories, and what blessings those are! Thank you also for the blessing of the power of a grace perspective!

The Miracle of a Miracle

We often use the word miracle merely to describe happenings of unexplainable luck or to give credence to happenings that have no physical or logical explanation. Scientists and skeptics (question marks) tend to debunk the existence of miracles by claiming that things which cannot be explained are merely happenings for which someone has yet to discover an answer. That definition of science is certainly true: the discovery of things that have always existed. Science has little room and no patience for faith and miracles, only for what it can prove.

I cannot help but chuckle when I witness, either on TV or in person, an evolutionist and creationist debating which theory can lay claim to the existence of humans on earth. Each side will espouse its merits of the argument, always leaving each other just a tad bit short of bridging the gap between theory and fact. That gap is why we have the theory of evolution and the theory of creation instead of the ability to explain the true facts of either. In the gap between theory and fact lies something that we know to exist in the natural world but also something that we cannot and never will have the capability to explain in the supernatural world: the miracle.

The miracle of a miracle is the requisite belief that miracles do indeed occur. Most times, belief in miracles arises from personal experiences or witnessing something otherwise inexplicable. Many other times, the belief in miracles merely flows from faith. Regardless, whether from experience, witness, or faith, just believing that miracles can and do occur will have a tremendous impact on one's perspective.

Just like in the story of Job, miracles affect our perspective of who controls events and why relying on faith is so crucial. My string of miracles not only saved me from the brink of death but also put into distinct terms the span of control that I have over my life and the span of control that God has over it. All my decisions and actions over a lifetime are in the realm of the little picture, what I can see that lies around and behind. God's actions, however, are in the realm of the big picture, including what lies ahead. Although God encourages us to reach forward to what lies ahead, only he can see what is there.

The first in my string of miracles is irrefutable evidence of God's ability to see what lies ahead. If you recall that particular experience, I had to make a decision on whether or not to proceed with my surgery while my wife Sherry was out of the country. I focused on what lay behind me: the information the doctors had told me a few days prior that the procedure would be a piece of cake. God, on the other hand, knew the possibility of what was lying ahead of me, spiraling down towards the brink of death. God could see that fate, but I could not. With that knowledge in mind, God needed to insert the miracle of my overwhelming feeling of **being alert** to every word spoken by the anesthetist and my need to ask questions about how this procedure may affect me. Through this miracle, I altered my initial instincts to go ahead with the surgery as planned for the next day and instead waited a week for Sherry to return. Had I proceeded, I more than likely would not have survived.

The author C.S. Lewis once described God's ability to see the big picture in the context of a sheet of paper.[11] The sheet of paper is our life, which to us appears in only two dimensions: length and width. Within the human two dimensions, we can subdivide the paper in many different ways to illustrate how we could view the flat sheet of paper from a two-dimensional perspective. C.S. Lewis illustrated this subdivision of a flat sheet of paper as containing a series of connected squares, but instead of squares, I would like to use words on a sheet of paper as my two-dimensional illustration.

From the beginning to the end of the sheet of paper are a series of words describing our life's story, past and present. We know what has transpired and is transpiring in our lives, but the two dimensions limit what we can see of the flat sheet of paper. Similar to the way we read a sheet of paper one word at a time, we also progress through our life's story one word at a time. We can see today and can remember what we have read in the past, but we must rely on faith and God's grace for what words of our life's story we cannot yet read.

God, on the other hand, does not see our life's story in two dimensions on a sheet of paper as we do, but in a multi-dimensional view where the flat sheet of paper is instead shaped and folded into a geometrical object. In God's view, our lives are multifaceted with many sides, each side having many possibilities and interconnected around a space in the center. Each of the facets can be multiple combinations of life stories with countless possibilities and outcomes depending on the choices that we make through our two-dimensional journey. We are in the center open space of the geometrical object, moving from side to side depending on our choices or actions, and God is on the outside looking at the entire object with a big picture view of the total sum of the possible outcomes. This view of all facets and outcomes gives God the ability to see forward via the big picture and even to communicate to us sometimes the outcomes of certain decisions or actions before we make a choice.

As I reflect through the subsequent miracles in my string of miracles, each instance can attest to God's ability to see forward via the big picture. In miracle number two, for example, my friend David felt compelled to walk back into the house at just the right moment to retrieve his cell phone when Sherry tried to reach him on his home phone line. Had he not obeyed that conscious impulse to return into the house, I again more than likely would not have survived. God, who knew the outcomes of David's actions with his ability to see the big picture, communicated to David that conscious thought to walk back into the house just as Sherry made the phone call.

Miracle after subsequent miracle in the string put the right person in the right place at just the right time to keep me from falling over the brink of death; such coordination depended upon God's view of the big picture. As God communicated to each individual his view of the possible outcomes, he manifested his presence in the form of a miracle. I believe with all my heart and soul that these happenings were not any mere set of coincidences, but miracles plain and simple.

The miracle of a miracle in terms of our perspective is the assurance that God can see what lies ahead in the realm of the big picture or what words are yet to be read, beyond our abilities. With that forward vision, God can intercede through the medium of a miracle. Whether or not the miracle will occur, as evidenced in my case, may depend on the decisions that we make to be alert or not, but our possible blindness does not diminish the miracle of a miracle.

A Grace Perspective Follows the Heart

I am not as smart or as tough or as self-sufficient as I once thought twenty or thirty years ago. Much of that attitude waned as I got older and came to grips with my vulnerability. I do remember the days of my late teens and early twenties, when I felt invincible and thus lived on the edge. Fortunately, I did not fall over the edge; I survived in spite of my attitude and perspective.

Those were carefree and fun filled days, but they were also empty and insecure days. During this early period of my life, I loved and lost in many relationships. I struggled through two divorces and several bouts of depression. I started my latter teens wanting to travel the world as a photo-journalist; then I wanted to be a linguist, then an engineer, then a professional photographer, all the while never stopping long enough to complete anything. I look back on those days and feel as though I drifted from person to person, place to place, and ideal to ideal.

This period of my life was also a time of rebellion against my father for hanging that balance sheet over my head like the sword of Damocles **(faith)**. I rebelled against religion as I felt it was corrupt **(cynicism)**, and I rebelled against God because I thought I could do just fine on my own **(arrogance)**. My perspective stank during this period, as I had a serious glass-half-empty view of life. Everywhere I went in everything I did, I saw no periods but plenty of question marks.

During this time of my life, my efforts never seemed to prove successful. Even in times of desperation when I put my arrogance momentarily aside and called to God, I felt as though he was not listening. Today I know that my feeling was not true. God was always listening, but while he was hearing my wails for help and guidance, he was also waiting. He was waiting for me to ask him not only to help, but also to become foremost in my life. The soul does not have enough room for both arrogance and grace; one or the other has to go. When I finally lost my grip on arrogance, God's grace began to fill the void, and my life has never been better.

Do I mean to imply that everything is now a bed of roses? Nope, no way, no how! God never promised me a smooth passage through life, but if I keep the faith, he will steer me to a safe landing at the end. As you have read in my story, my life has included plenty of ups and downs, and more of both lie ahead. The difference between my days of arrogance and my days of God's grace is that now, no matter what, everything always seems to resolve beneficially. In matters of family, finance, or work, no matter how glum a situation may appear at first, it ends better than I had first hoped. Sometimes I have to pinch myself, because the resolution seems a bit surreal, but it is the miracle of God's grace and its amazing impact on the power of my grace perspective.

I have been noticing from time to time a pompous atheist author who has been making quite a good living lately doing the talk show and anti-religion speaking circuit, debunking the existence of God and faith. As unnerving and annoying as this person is, he is also worthy of much pity. Of the numerous times that I have seen him on talk shows and cable TV spewing his acerbic rhetoric, not once have I ever witnessed him smile. Just a plain and simple smile escapes him! That lack alone is pitiful, and it shows what a lousy perspective he must have.

Watching him, I have also gained a sense that what is closest to his heart is intelligence (he is very intelligent) and self-reliance. He may be convinced that intelligence and self-reliance are all that is necessary to sustain his perspective. Unfortunately for him, in spite of his intellect, he is severely deficient in perspective.

Intellect has become one the greatest conveyances for arrogance and cynicism. Intellect has also become a convenient substitute for faith. Mind you, there is absolutely nothing wrong with intelligence. In fact, God never discourages us from learning and becoming as intelligent as we can, as long as the sum total of our intelligence does not obscure truth.

Reliance on intellect, wealth, power, career, or a plethora of other things such as artificial substances, as I know firsthand, is shallow and finite. Such reliance has nothing solid with which to sustain the spirit, and so it can also come to an abrupt end. At the end of a life journey, coming face to face with a perspective full of question marks must be a hellish experience. A journey ending that way has nothing but unanswered questions and unrealized opportunities. I cannot imagine my journey not mattering in the end the same way as those who have nothing worthwhile to remember.

Regardless of the perceived accomplishments, finality and shallowness contain a vacuum called missed opportunities of grace. I wish that question mark people could just take a grace pill to experience however briefly what a perspective based on grace and unconditional love can be like. I would be willing to bet that more than just a few perspectives would change. In the end, however, that pill would violate God's insistence on allowing us the free will to make our own decisions.

"Wherever your treasure is, there your heart [and your perspective] will be also" (Matthew 6:21). The key to that perspective is whether the heart is following something that is finite and shallow or something that is eternal. Everything in life between your first and last breath comes to an end. Youth comes and goes; wealth comes and goes; careers come and go; relationships come and go; the euphoria from drugs and alcohol come and go. Everything of the physical world follows the same pattern. So people who have allowed their hearts to follow something that has no permanence moan, groan, and lament about what was or what could have been. I have been there and done that, and I never care to go there again.

On the other hand, I prefer to smile, laugh, and anticipate life. Although my perspective has changed over the decades, my recent experiences at the brink of death have only solidified my resolve to keep my heart's treasure where I know it belongs, in what was there before my first breath and will be there long after I take my last one: God. Life is less complex and less stressful when you stand shoulder to shoulder with God rather than all alone. A simple smile is all the evidence that you will ever need to verify it.

Chapter 15

Coming Full Circle – the NEW Beginning

I love circles. To me, circles are the most intriguing and, at the same time, the most mysterious of all geometric shapes. Whenever we place things into the realm of eternity, we always refer to circles. For example; a person who is "going in circles" never finds an answer; love is a "never ending circle," means the same as love is eternal; "a circle of friends," indicates relationships that we consider permanent, and so on.

"Coming full circle" is a phrase which also has its roots in permanence. When one has come full circle, he comes back to the point from which he started. However, no reference to coming full circle applies to reaching an end, because a circle can have infinite beginnings and not one single ending. Just draw a circle on a piece of paper. The point from which you begin to draw a circle can be its beginning point, but once you have closed the circle, where is the end? It has none!

Once a circle is complete, it becomes never ending. You can even draw a small period to intersect at any point on a circle, trace around the circle back to the point from which you started tracing, and still you will see no end to the circle. You will only come full circle to the point from which you started. Keep drawing periods around your circle and tracing full circles from each point, and soon you will have a circle full of many beginnings without one single ending.

Continue to make intersection periods and traces around your circle; do you begin to pass previous periods that you have made? Have you ever had a feeling of deja vu? As you make more periods and traces, you will pass over previous ones. These repetitions also make circles and coming full circle so intriguing. Each of our lives is a single circle. The circles will have many points of beginning but not one point of ending. The multitude of period points of beginning leave a residue of recollection that we will observe from time to time, causing us to reflect on having been there before. And you have!

Coming full circle to periods in our lives passes many times without notice, but specific events **mark** other times. That unusually cool August Sunday, four months after I woke from the brink of death to the wonderful experiences that God had in store, **marked** my life circle. That circle started in the baptismal in Jeffersonville, Indiana and came full circle in another baptismal in Lawrence, Kansas. The event that created the **mark** of my coming full circle was the testimony that I gave to the family, friends, and congregation in attendance describing my forty-three year journey from baptismal to baptismal and how God was by my side every step of the way. I would like to share that testimony with you:

Marking the Circle with a Testimony

Thank you, Pastor, and good morning to you all. At the end of the service today, I have the privilege of sharing with my many friends and family in atten-

dance this morning and you, my church family, a very special moment for me from both a personal and a spiritual perspective: the renewal of my commitment and faith in our God and his Son through baptism. But first I am also privileged to share my story and testimony about the road that has brought me here to this day and its events.

Just a second ago, I mentioned the fact that this baptism is a renewal, because you see this is not the first time that I was baptized. My story and testimony begins with the first baptism.

I'd like to take you all back in time forty-three years ago to the town of Jeffersonville, Indiana, on the banks of the Ohio River, where as a young boy of nine I was baptized for the first time in a tiny church called the Branham Tabernacle. The circumstances that brought me to the baptismal that Sunday morning in 1962 are the first part of my testimony and also a set of circumstances that have haunted me for many years.

You see, I was raised in a faith environment of fear. The religion that I came to know as a child was one of retribution and consequence rather than love and forgiveness. I was always led to believe that God would punish me for whatever I may have done wrong, whether in the faith of the church or against its doctrines.

I heard, "Don't do this," or "Don't do that because God will punish you." Or if something bad did happen to me, I heard, "See, I told you God would punish you." Those were the mantras of my early childhood.

This instilled fear of God was what brought me to baptism for the first time. Our church taught that, if you were not baptized and baptized in the name of Jesus Christ instead of the name of the Father, Son, and Holy Spirit, you would burn in hell for all eternity. That's a pretty compelling argument for a nine year-old kid already in a state of religious paranoia, and it formed the impetus of why I was baptized. I was scared of what would happen to me if I was not. I had no classes on faith and baptism prior to that Sunday morning's service, only fear and urgency of getting it done so that I could have a feeling of relief that I was safe after it was over. That sense of safety, however, turned into a feeling of emptiness as I grew older.

Fortunately, as I began to grow and mature into adulthood, I eventually discovered that the doctrine of retribution and consequence that I was taught to believe as a child was a false one. Through perseverance and faith, I rightfully discovered that God is a loving, caring, and merciful God, not a God that is vindictive. He was not out to get me when I made a mistake, but loved me just as I am, faults and all.

Let's fast forward now to April 12, 2005, a date which brings me to the second part of my story and testimony. As many of you know, just a few short months ago, I faced the greatest challenge that I or anyone else could ever face, fighting for my life. If there were a video screen up on the wall right now that could peer back to where I was exactly four months ago, you would see a person in grave condition lying in an Intensive Care Unit in Kansas City hooked to a ventilator, which was the only thing that was keeping me alive.

I do not want to belabor the details of how I came to be in such a grave state, but I do want to mention that the circumstances that placed me there were both sudden and unexpected. What was supposed to be a simple procedure involving a two or three day stay in the hospital turned into ten days in ICU, ten more days in the Cardiovascular Unit, and many, many more weeks of convalescing and recovery at home.

So what does this crisis have to do with the baptism today? Well, first of all, I'm not here as part of a deal that I made with God. When I woke at the end of my ten days in ICU, I did no plead, "God, let me live, and I'll do whatever you want me to do." No there was none of that. I don't mean that I wasn't afraid of dying, because I was. In fact, I had never experienced such fear, even as a child when I was taught to fear.

But my fear quickly subsided, because almost immediately after my first prayers to God to spare me from death had left my lips, I was suddenly surrounded by a warm sensation of assurance reminiscent of the promise in Matthew 28:16-20 to have no fear because "surely I am with you always, even until the end of the age." I was no longer afraid, because from that moment on, I knew that I was in good hands.

So, the reason why I am here today to recommit and renew my faith in Jesus Christ is the combination of filling the emptiness left in the wake of my first baptism forty-three years ago coupled with thanking

God for the experiences that he blessed me to have, starting in the hospital four months ago and continuing through today.

Yes, you did hear me right; I did say that what happened to me in the hospital was a blessing. You may be asking yourself: How can he possibly equate nearly losing his life and the resulting challenges since then as a blessing? Well, what happened to me four months ago opened my eyes and reminded me of three things that I had always known to be true but kept filed away in the back of my spiritual filing cabinet until April of 2005.

First of all, my battle with death reminded me of how fragile and how short our time on earth really is. We've all kept in the back of our minds the truth that, yeah, someday we are going to die, and then we file that thought away. But believe me, when you've been on the brink of death and even beyond, that reality suddenly comes to prominence in the forefront of everything you do.

The second thing about which my battle with death reminded me was that God is truly with us always. Since I woke up in the ICU, I have lost count of how many times someone has asked, "Well, did you see a bright light?" They each assume an expression of utter disappointment when I respond with a resounding, "No, I did not." I'm not sure if those who have asked this question are looking for an assurance or affirmation that God really does exist or if they feel disappointment at my response for some other reason, but every time I am taken aback by their empty looks.

No, I did not see a light, but I can assure you today standing in front of you in this house of the Lord that he is real and with us every minute of the day. His assurance to me after my prayers to him on that day I woke from my ten days of unconsciousness spoke more volumes of his existence than any light could ever produce. You see, God did not need to send a light to assure me of his presence, because he loved me enough to be there in person. And if that presence isn't a blessed assurance of his existence, then I don't know what else to say.

God also surrounded me with his angels both heavenly and earthly to reassure me of his presence as well. Yes, I did say earthly angels. For I fervently believe that the good works we do in his name to help others make us all his angels. All of you prayed for me while I fought to stay alive. Craig, Sally Don, and their kids brought us dinner the first few nights after I got home to help Sherry, who had her hands full and needed a break. My father-in-law Richard sat with me every day while I was unconscious and brought me coffee from QuickTrip each morning after I woke up. My sister Rosie, who is a nurse, made sure that the nurses tending to me were doing their best to care for me. My lifelong friend David stood diligently over me as the doctors were having difficulty diagnosing my condition. My two boys, Jon and Matt, remained strong and comforted their mom through the whole ordeal, and my bride Sherry was by my side the whole time. You see, each and every one of you is an angel from God that he sent to help me pull through my struggle. God bless all of you, and thank you for being his angels for me.

The third and last thing of which my battle with death reminded me was that every second of every day is a blessing from God. We can take credit for nothing under the sun and stars, because without God's abundant blessings we are nothing but dust. Every breath that I take, every step that I make, and every hand that I shake is literally a blessing from God, and now more than ever I give the credit to him for all that I have been, what I am now, and if it is within his will, what I will be in the future.

Hopefully, now you can see why my whole ordeal of being on the brink of death was a blessing from God: because it has caused me to see myself and my purpose in life from a whole new perspective. The reminder of how frail and short life is puts a sense of purpose in all that I do. I now look at what I used to consider as mundane tasks as an opportunity to do better, because I may not have a chance to do them again. When I'm walking down the street or driving through the neighborhood and see someone that I have not seen for a long time, I don't smile, wave, and move on anymore. Now I stop, turn around, and spend a little time just talking to that person, because who knows if I'll ever see him again.

I also find myself looking up a lot and just saying thanks, sometimes before a meal, sometimes during a walk with my dog Katie, and sometimes just after taking a deep breath. With God all around me, it feels good to take a big lung full of him inside and just say thanks for bringing me back.

> *So today, my road comes full circle from that Sunday morning forty-three years ago in Jeffersonville, Indiana. Even though I have hit a few bumps along the way, I would never hesitate to travel the same road again, because during my entire journey I am comforted by the fact that I have never been alone. God has always been with me and will continue to be with me, even until the end of the age.*
>
> *Thank you for allowing me to share my story and testimony with you this morning, and may God bless you with a journey on your road through life as wonderful as mine.*

A few moments later, I glanced up at the cross that I had visualized so many times while lying in the hospital, and I walked down the steps into the warm water. The Pastor then followed a ritual in our church in which he asks each candidate for baptism before immersion to proclaim his faith publicly by declaring, "Jesus Christ is Lord." Once I made that proclamation, the Pastor cupped my hands over my nose and mouth and immersed me into the water saying, "We are buried in death with Christ," and then he pulled me out of the water and said, "And are raised with him to walk in the newness of life." After forty-three years of wandering in spirit and faith, this point in my life **marked** my coming full circle. Now was the time to place a **period** at a new beginning!

In my journey, I experienced the truth that life is complex, full of stress, and full of anxiety. In past times, the more complexity I faced, the more stressful and anxious I became, and the more my perspective would suffer. Rather than having periods in my circles, I had too many question marks which left no place to mark coming full circle and beginning anew. Many of you reading this book may feel the same.

What is so ironic is that for all the mucking up of life, for all the ambiguity of spirituality and faith, there is a simple answer, grace! And the source of that grace is the unconditional love of the giver of grace, God.

Do you have your doubts? Then ask yourself this simple question. What is the most important thing in your life? Now think about your answer. There is no sin or shame in wealth, possessions, careers, or the many things we may enjoy in life, only the void created by putting these things above all else. Nothing finite can sustain the spirit; only grace can.

Grace does not require you to cast off anything that is important to you, only to reorder your priorities. Once the priorities are reordered, then your perspective begins to come into line as well. I promise you an amazing personal transformation, and if you have not yet experienced it, I hope that you will.

One last critical factor remains though, and that is the issue of time. Just like all physical things, time is a finite resource as well. Time is of the essence for you to reorder your life and your perspective. To waste an entire life or even one more day without experiencing what grace can do for you and your perspective would be a shame.

If you need help or are unsure of what to do next, open your eyes, be alert, and look around you. Many people of faith with great perspectives are all around, and places of worship can guide you towards experiencing the joy of grace, new beginnings, and most importantly, a new perspective on your life..

Through God's grace on your perspective, you can forget what lies behind, as your past will not be fatal, and reach forward to what lies ahead, as your future will never be final.

May God bless you and your perspective.

Endnotes

1. Ursula K. Le Guin, *The Left Hand of Darkness* (New York: Ace Books, 1969), 220.
2. John Lennon and Paul McCartney, "The Ballad of John and Yoko," single release © 1969 Apple Records.
3. Dr. Patrick Morley, as cited in Bruce Bickel and Stan Jantz, *Evidence for Faith101: Understanding Apologetics in Plain Language* (Eugene, OR: Harvest House, 2008), 144.
4. Dr. Martin Luther King, Jr., "I Have a Dream" (speech at the March on Washington for Jobs and Freedom in Washington, D.C., August 28, 1963).
5. C.S. Lewis, *Mere Christianity,* 3rd ed. (New York: Harper Collins, 1952), 68.
6. Ibid., 67.
7. Bobby McFerrin, "Don't Worry, Be Happy" on *Don't Worry, Be Happy* © 1988 EMI.
8. Randy J. Larsen and David M. Buss, *Personality Psychology: Domains of Knowledge About Human Nature,* 3rd ed. (New York: McGraw-Hill, 2008), 332-333.
9. *Wikipedia*, s.v. "Serenity Prayer," http://en.wikipedia.org/wiki/Serenity_prayer (accessed January 20, 2011).
10. Tim Keller (as cited in Bickel and Jantz, 260-261).
11. Lewis, 139.